December/83

To Jules

From John & Louise

Working with Wood

Mike Lawrence

Working with Wood

David & Charles
Newton Abbot   London

This book was created, designed and
produced by Reference International,
21 Soho Square, London, in association
with Martensson Books, London

Executive editor Wendy Martensson
Editor William Fried
Design Julian Holland
Photography Chris Overton, Richard
Mummery .
Photo research Alice Baker
Illustrations Sutton/Paddock, Don
Parry

ISBN 0 7153 7828 7

© 1979 Reference International Publishers Ltd

Published in the United States
by Thomas Y. Crowell
New York, 1979

Published in the United Kingdom by
David & Charles, Brunel House,
Newton Abbot, 1979

Printed in the United States

Contents

Introduction

Working with Wood is designed as a basic woodworking manual and a guide to the skills of traditional and modern woodworking. It is both a useful reference book and a workshop handbook. It introduces the tools needed for home woodworking – both hand and power tools – and explains how they are used, cared for and stored.

Working with Wood presents the types of wood which are generally available, the purposes for which each is best suited and explains how to select wood, spot defects, and how to get wood home and store it there. It includes useful information on gluing and on woodworking joints from simple edge and dowel joints to the more complex mortise and tenon and dovetail joints.

The book also introduces techniques for working with man-made sheet materials such as plywood, particle board and hardboard and includes a selection of things to make for your workshop from a bench hook to a professional woodworking bench. The instructions throughout are illustrated with detailed line drawings and photographs.

Working with Wood takes the mystery out of the tools and techniques of woodworking and sets you well on the path to becoming a professional.

Working with wood

Wood was one of the first materials man turned to when he needed tools and utensils. It was readily available and comparatively easy to fashion into the shape he wanted even with the most primitive of tools. And it was durable enough for his everyday needs. It made bowls for his food, simple enclosures for his livestock, a roof over his head and some simple furniture for his wooden house. And as he made all these things, he learned the rudiments of working with wood—how to cut it, shape it and join it together.

In many ways the art of working with wood hasn't changed much over the centuries. Archaeologists have unearthed evidence of woodworking from ancient Egypt assembled with joints that we would recognize today and tools from Roman settlements that bear a striking resemblance to their modern counterparts, both in principle and in design.

The reason why things have changed so little is that wood itself is unchanging. The success with which it is worked depends most of all on the craftsman's understanding of the way in which it has grown. Used with skill and an understanding of its properties, it can serve an almost limitless range of purposes.

The early woodworker had a hard life getting the wood he needed. He couldn't buy his wood ready shaped for him to use. He had to cut it himself. After felling the tree he had chosen, he and an assistant sawed the log into beams or boards with an upright two-man saw.

It was strenuous work, but there was no other way of doing the job except with a few woods like oak that could be split by driving wedges into the ends and sides of the log. Apart from being much quicker than sawing, this method had the advantage that splitting the wood exactly along the grain left it stronger than sawn wood. It did mean, however, that the wood was seldom very straight, which accounts for the irregularity of much old woodwork.

To trim the wood to shape once it was cut or split, the woodworker used a tool called an adze. He stood over his work and swung the adze downward and toward his feet, removing the wood in chips to leave a surface of scalloped facets. A skilled craftsman could make the surface remarkably smooth.

Then he turned to the rest of his tools—planes, chisels, saws, drills and hammers—to fashion the wood into the precise shape he wanted. The only machine he had at his disposal was the lathe powered by a treadle, which enabled him to produce rounded sections of wood.

Workers in wood were named according to the work in which they specialized. The man who carried out structural woodwork or made carts in the early Middle Ages was called a wright. The latin word carpentum means a cart or wain, hence generations of Carpenters, Cartwrights and Wainwrights scattered throughout the English-speaking world. Joiners came later, as makers of fittings and simple furniture, practicing an art "whereby several Pieces of Wood are so fitted and joined together that they shall seeme an intire Piece," as one seventeenth century writer described joinery to his readers. Gradually the joiner became a cabinetmaker—the producer of fine pieces of furniture.

Early furniture was made of solid wood, joined together roughly. Thinner panels made lighter furniture, but tended to split and so were held in sturdy frameworks, the forerunners of the panelled furniture of today. Veneering, known to the Egyptians, became popular again as a way of displaying the beauty of the wood grain in a manner that could not be achieved with solid wood. Travelers brought back new woods from the countries they visited, and carving and intricate inlay work led to new, more ornate furniture styles. In this century man learned to overcome one of the problems of natural wood—that you could not have a piece longer than a tree was tall nor wider than its trunk's diameter. He made boards by slicing up and grinding down the raw material and assembling it into large sheets. With these he was able to do away with frame construction almost entirely, making simple box-like furniture with hardly a joint in sight.

Today, machines have to a large extent replaced the woodworker's skills. The only hope that the craft will survive lies in the individual, who enjoys working with wood in the quiet of his own workshop, creating the things he wants from the woods he likes best, in the manner his skills and his tools will allow.

CHAPTER 1
The raw material

Everyone must be familiar with the characteristic cross section of a tree. If you look closely you will learn a lot about how a tree grows. The first things you will notice are the rings, spreading outward from the center to the bark like ripples on a pond. The inner part of the log, called the heartwood, provides the strong structural backbone of the tree. The outer layers, called the sapwood, carry water and dissolved mineral salts—the sap—up from the roots to the branches and leaves. Each year, during the summer growing season, the tree grows a new layer of wood on the outside of the sapwood layer. Because more sap rises through the sapwood during spring than during summer, the new wood cells formed in spring are larger. It is the difference in size, and therefore color, between the spring and summer wood that causes alternate light and dark rings. These are called annual rings because of the yearly growth cycle that produces them.

To the woodworker, the difference between sapwood and heartwood is of considerable importance. The heartwood, being composed of older cells that are no longer growing, is relatively dense and stable when it is cut from the log. By contrast, the sapwood is much softer, more liable to warp and more prone to attack by wood-boring insects and wood-destroying fungi. Much modern wood is cut from fast-growing trees like pine, so the rings are widely spaced. It is cut when the tree is still young, so it contains a lot of sapwood and not much heartwood. That is why it is more prone to warping and decay than wood cut from older trees or from species which grow more slowly.

Hardwood and softwood
Wood is divided botanically into two distinct groups, called hardwoods and softwoods. However, these names are not a guide to whether the wood is soft or hard to work. Balsa, for example, is one of the softest woods we know, and yet is technically a hardwood, while yew, a dense wood that is quite difficult to work, is characterized as a softwood.

The name softwood is applied to the family of cone-bearing or evergreen trees, such as pine, spruce, fir and larch, which grow in a well-defined belt running around the northern hemisphere from northern Britain across the Baltic countries and Russia to Canada. Some species of softwood also grow at high altitude in the tropics, but in relatively small quantities. The greatest reserves of softwood are found in Canada, Scandinavia, and in Russia, particularly Siberia.

Hardwood is the generic term for deciduous trees, those that lose their leaves in autumn. They usually grow in warmer climates than the softwoods. Hardwoods include such familiar species as ash, beech, elm, mahogany, oak, teak and walnut, and a whole host of less common names: idigbo, iroko, meranti and muninga, for example. Apart from the native European and American species, the biggest sources of wood supply are West Africa, the West Indies and Southeast Asia.

When you go to buy wood, you will find hardwoods sold by name, though some varieties may be passed off as other more expensive ones because of similarities in color and grain pattern. But life is not so easy when you are shopping for softwood. It is rarely sold by species. It is divided fairly arbitrarily into two groups, probably because there is less variation in color and grain between the softwood varieties than there is with hardwoods. The first group is known variously as redwood, pine, red deal or yellow deal. There is no such thing as a deal tree; deal originally meant a piece of sawn fir or pine of a certain size. The second group is called whitewood, or is occasionally marked up as spruce, hemlock or some other species. It is best known as the traditional Christmas tree.

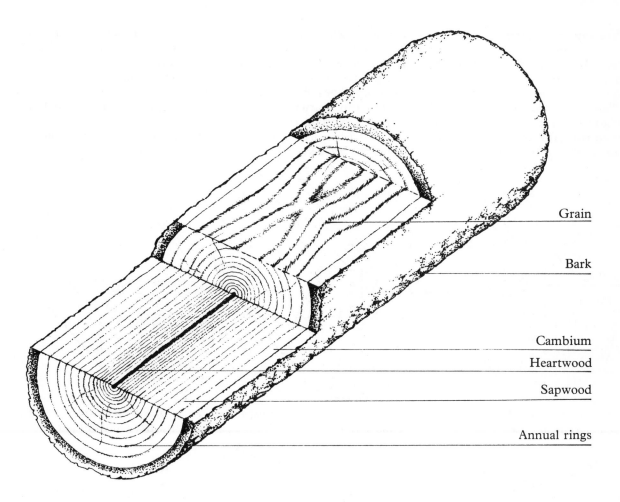

Grain

Bark

Cambium

Heartwood

Sapwood

Annual rings

The drawing above shows in cutaway form the various parts of a log. Outermost is the bark, a protective layer formed between spring and summer each year by the cells of the cambium layer beneath it. The cambium layer forms new sapwood cells each year too, so the tree grows as new wood and bark are formed around its circumference. The sapwood forms the bulk of the tree's cross section, and consists of layers of living cells through which moisture is carried up the tree from the roots. Inside the sapwood is the heartwood layer, made up of inactive cells of a darker color. As the tree gets larger, the inner layers of sapwood turn into heartwood. Each year's growth cycle adds further annual rings—a pale, wide ring is formed by fast-growing spring cells and a narrow, darker ring is formed by the smaller, slower-growing summer cells. The grain of the wood is the pattern these rings make when the wood is cut horizontally across the log and is used to identify species.

11

Sawing up the logs

Conversion is the woodworker's term for sawing up the logs in such a way as to produce the greatest quantity of good quality wood. Plain sawing is the quickest and cheapest method, yielding planks with two different grain patterns, according to their position in the log from which they are cut. Those cut from the edge of the log have a distinct tendency to curl and warp as sapwood is less stable than heartwood. The only way of avoiding this is to quarter saw the log. This method produces more stable wood which has an attractive grain.

Once the log has been sawn, it is seasoned at a controlled rate to dry out the sap, thereby reducing the moisture content of the wood. Seasoning not only makes the wood easier to work, lighter to handle and less prone to fungal attack, but carefully seasoned wood is also less likely to warp and shrink than unseasoned wood.

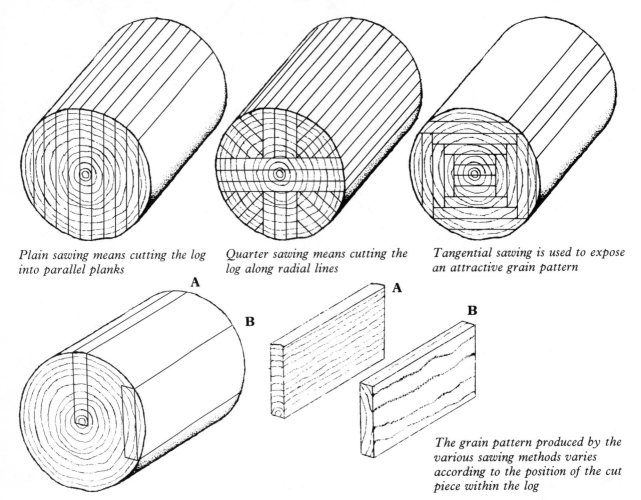

Plain sawing means cutting the log into parallel planks

Quarter sawing means cutting the log along radial lines

Tangential sawing is used to expose an attractive grain pattern

The grain pattern produced by the various sawing methods varies according to the position of the cut piece within the log

Faults in wood

The unique qualities that make wood such an attractive material to work with can also cause problems for the woodworker. As a growing thing, wood has peculiarities and defects in its growth that can affect its strength and appearance. One of the most obvious is the knot, which is the cross section of a branch exposed in sawing at the point where it starts growing from the trunk. The knot may still be fresh or live and tight-fitting in the surrounding wood, perhaps even oozing resin. Or it may be dark and dead. This is a sign that the branch was damaged before the tree was felled.

Live knots cause few problems, as long as they are not too close together. They can even be an attractive feature of the wood's appearance, although they may need careful treatment if they're not to mar the look of any finish you want to give the wood. Dead knots, on the other hand, can cause trouble because they tend to shrink and fall out, leaving a hole in the wood which weakens it and which will have to be plugged or filled.

Another type of fault which occurs after the tree has been felled, but before it is sawn up, is a split, called a "shake" by woodworkers. A star shake results when the outside of the log dries and shrinks more quickly than the heart, and leads to splits running across the log on the outside of the wood. A cup shake occurs when the inner part of the log shrinks more rapidly than the outer part. The end result is a separation of the wood between adjacent annual rings. A thunder shake, a cracking along the grain, is caused by careless felling or handling of the log. African mahogany suffers particularly from this fault. An end shake is a split in the ends of pieces of sawn wood caused by their being dried out too quickly during seasoning. This is a common fault and something you should look for when you buy wood. The ends can of course be cut off, but the waste can be expensive.

Warping is caused by uneven drying of the sawn wood, and can lead to a cup shake, bow or a twist.

You may also find what is really a blemish rather than a defect in the wood, a staining or discoloration caused either by attack from various fungi or by bad storage. This doesn't weaken the wood, but it can spoil its appearance.

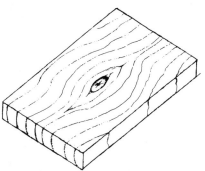

Knots are the cross sections of branches on the tree

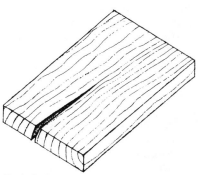

End shakes are splits caused by too rapid seasoning

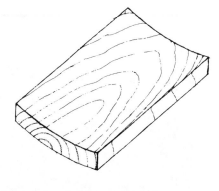

Warping, caused by uneven drying, gives the wood a cupped shape

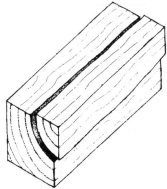

Cup shakes lead to splits along the grain line inside the wood

Characteristics of wood

There are such wide variations in the color, grain pattern and working properties of wood that a few words about the species you are likely to find will be useful. First, softwoods, which are used for much general carpentry work and joinery around the house.

DOUGLAS FIR, COLUMBIAN PINE
Both of these woods are reddish-brown in color, with a grain pattern that is quite pronounced and may be slightly wavy. The wood is almost free of knots, comes in wide boards and is easy to work. For this reason it is used extensively in paneling.

HEMLOCK
Pale yellow, even slightly gray in color, with a straight grain and moderately fine texture. It is strong, but not very resistant to decay, and is used for general-purpose indoor work.

REDWOOD, PINE, RED/YELLOW DEAL
Light reddish-brown or yellow-brown color, usually straight-grained but fairly resinous. Takes nails and screws well, and is widely used for general carpentry and joinery work.

WHITEWOOD, SPRUCE
A very pale wood, usually with a straight if unpronounced grain pattern and even texture. It is fairly strong, but is prone to decay, and is used for indoor work only.

PARANA PINE
The one softwood from the southern hemisphere, mainly Brazil, this wood has a pleasant light to dark brown color with characteristic red streaks. It is used mainly for indoor furniture, and is easy to work, but tends to split when nailed. The grain is straight and virtually knot-free. Most useful of all, it is available in widths of up to 12 in. (305mm).

WESTERN RED CEDAR
A light, brown-colored wood, best known for its resistance to weathering and wood-boring insects, a property due to a natural oil present in the wood. It does not twist or warp even when exposed to heat, but bruises easily and is not a strong wood for structural use.

Now some of the hardwoods, which are used almost exclusively to make fine furniture.

AFRORMOSIA
A brownish-yellow wood from West Africa, often considered as a substitute for teak. Unfortunately it tends to change color on exposure to light, and is oily and difficult to work.

ASH
A European and North American wood, pale yellow in color and with a fairly straight grain. It is tough and bends well without splitting, a useful property for making bent-wood furniture and for framing work.

BEECH
A fine-textured European wood, pink to yellow-brown in color and usually straight-grained. It is easy to work, and takes nails and tacks particularly well, so it is widely used for the frames of upholstered furniture and for cabinet carcasses.

The characteristic grain pattern of sycamore (above left), oak (above right), mahogany (below left) and ash (below right)

ELM

A distinctively grained wood with a light brown color, strong, durable and fairly resistant to decay. It warps badly, though, and is not easy to work.

IDIGBO

A West African tree whose wood ranges from pale yellow to light brown in color. It is easily worked, but has a fairly coarse texture.

IROKO

Another West African tree, similar in appearance to teak, but very hard and coarse-grained. It darkens gradually on exposure to light, eventually turning almost black.

MAHOGANY

A mid-red wood with an attractive grain pattern, one of the finest cabinetmaking woods. African varieties are darker in color than those from Central America.

MERANTI

Similar in appearance to mahogany, though more coarse-grained. Be careful not to buy wood damaged by hole-boring insects; it can be wasteful if a lot of wood has to be cut out.

OAK

European oak is extremely strong and dense, and is rather hard to work. Its open grained structure is often filled before finishing. It is an acidic wood and attacks steel nails and screws, causing rust marks. For this reason brass screws are usually used on oak furniture. American and Japanese oak is less well marked.

RAMIN

A straight-grained wood of a uniform color, extensively used for picture framing and small moldings.

ROSEWOOD

A rich brown wood with a beautiful grain pattern, more often used as a veneer nowadays.

SAPELE

Similar to mahogany, characterized by a marked and regular stripe. Difficult to plane because of its irregular grain.

TEAK

One of the most durable hardwoods, it varies in grain and color from clear gold to dark brown. It is hard to work, however, and is also very oily, which makes gluing and finishing difficult. The best choice for outdoor furniture, where it weathers to an attractive gray color if left untreated.

UTILE

Similar in appearance to sapele, it is easy to work and resists decay well. One of the most popular hardwoods.

WALNUT

A rich brown color and an attractive curling grain pattern, excellent to work and takes a good finish.

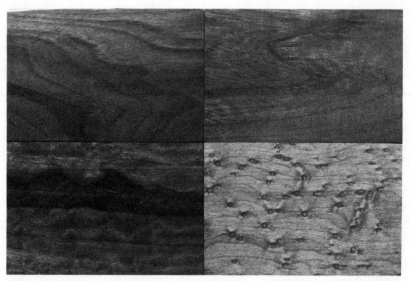

More beautiful grain patterns—walnut (above left), elm (above right) cedar (below left) and bird's eye maple (below right)

Qualities of wood

Because wood is a natural material, its quality is distinctly variable; even a single log can contain some perfect wood and some areas that are so damaged, decayed or otherwise substandard they are almost useless except for the roughest work. For this reason wood is sorted into grades when it leaves the sawmill, and again into categories when it reaches the retailer. Some suppliers sell wood by the sawmill grades, which can be confusing when you buy it.

Sawmill grades tend to vary according to the country from which the wood has been imported. For example, softwood from Scandinavia and Russia is often divided into two broad categories, called "unsorted" and "fifths." Unsorted is the better quality. It is a misleading term since it means that all the poorer quality wood has already been removed. Wood from Canada is usually divided into "clears" and "merchantable" grades. The clears are of better quality than the Russian and Scandinavian unsorted grade. Parana pine, the only softwood imported from Brazil, is often graded into No. 1 and No. 2, both of which are as good as the best grade of Canadian wood.

However, suppliers who sort their wood further when they receive it from the importer or the sawmill make life easier, by regrading the stock into three grades called best joinery, joinery and carcassing or building grade.

Best joinery is top quality wood, likely to be virtually knot-free and suitable for the finest finish where the grain and color will be visible. Standard joinery grade is ideal for general woodworking. The carcassing or building grade, which is usually sold only as sawn boards, is used for all structural work and for frameworks, battens and the like where the wood will be hidden from view.

In America the best grades are called Firsts and Seconds, or 1 and 2 clear, C select and D select. Wood of poorer quality than this is called common lumber, and is graded from No. 1 common, the best grade, down to No. 5, the least desirable. No. 2 common is sometimes referred to as construction grade and No. 4 common as utility grade. Clear lumber is wood free of knots, and the best choice for work that will be given a natural finish. Grades from C down to No. 2 common are suitable for most interior and exterior work that will be painted. No. 2 common in particular is used for knotty pine paneling. No. 4 common is the equivalent of the British carcassing grade, and is used for general structural work.

Whatever grading system is in use at your local supplier, make sure you understand what the various grades mean before you buy. If you are in any doubt, ask.

These grades are usually applied only to softwoods. Hardwoods are rarely graded, because it is understood by supplier and customer that the wood will be chosen for its color and grain pattern, and therefore only the hardwood equivalent of a softwood best joinery or clear lumber grade will be acceptable. Hardwood is usually sold sawn for larger sections, planed all around for smaller ones.

Sizes

Both softwood and hardwood are sold in a wide range of standard sizes. These are either produced to metric sizes, measured in millimeters, or in inches and fractions of an inch. To convert one system to the other, remember that 25mm equals one inch—an accurate enough conversion except for large measurements—or buy a steel tape (page 34) marked with both inches and millimeters, and read off the equivalent measurements from that.

The most important thing to remember about the size of wood when you buy it is that the sizes quoted are nominal, not actual. The wood is sawn to a given size, but it shrinks during seasoning, and may then also be planed to produce a smoother surface, which reduces the actual size of the wood still further. Some mills remove more wood in planing than others, but on average you can reckon that planed wood will be at least $\frac{1}{8}$ in. (3mm) smaller overall than the nominal size, and may be even more undersize on larger cross sections.

Nominal thicknesses of both hardwood and softwood start at $\frac{1}{2}$ in. (12mm). Other standard thicknesses are $\frac{5}{8}$ in. (15mm), $\frac{3}{4}$ in. (18mm), $\frac{7}{8}$ in. (22mm), 1 in. (25mm), $1\frac{1}{4}$ in. (32mm), $1\frac{1}{2}$ in. (38mm), 2 in. (50mm), and then upwards in 1 in. (25mm) steps to about 4 in. (100mm). You are unlikely to want wood that is any thicker than this.

Widths follow a similar sequence up to 2 in. (50mm); from there they go up in 1 in. (25mm) steps to 9 in. (225mm) and occasionally to 12 in. (305mm) for the widest boards. Lengths vary widely—the shortest piece of wood you can reasonably expect to buy is one foot, and for longer pieces it is usual to buy in multiples of this. You can't expect whoever is selling you the wood to price it to any smaller unit. If you are buying metric units, watch out for anyone rigorously using the so-called metric foot of 300mm instead of the true foot of 305mm. On long lengths you could find your piece a critical fraction short.

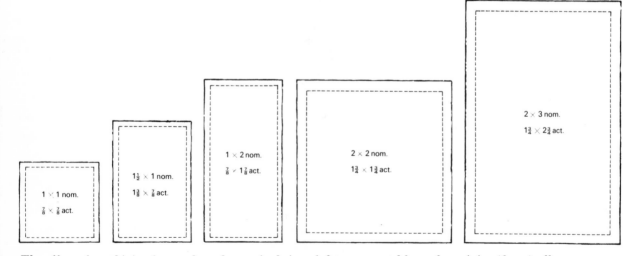

The effect of machining is to reduce the nominal size of the sawn wood by at least $\frac{1}{8}$ in. (3mm) all around, as shown in these representative sections

Special sections

Most of the wood you buy and use will be simple square and rectangular sections. But there are times when you want wood in a particular shape for a special purpose. Once you would have had to shape it yourself, but now you can buy wood that has been planed and milled into just about every shape under the sun. These special sections known as moldings are used for one of three reasons.

First, to match some existing woodwork, the opening casement of a window, for example. Special window moldings are produced, called stiles, rails and glazing bars. Or you may need some new archi-trave molding, the elaborate framing around a door opening, to match the one you already have.

Second, you may want a molding for a special task—carrying a pair of sliding closet doors, for example, or framing a picture. Finally, you may simply want a molding as a decoration on the piece you are making, either in its own right or as a clever way of masking a join, where wooden wall panels turn an internal or external corner, for example. Big suppliers carry a large stock of different molding sections. So whether it's for a window sill, an architrave, a cornice, a handrail for your stairs, or a picture frame, you should be able to find the one you want.

Incidentally, with the exception of having a choice between hardwood and softwood window sill moldings, all the larger moldings are machined from softwood, and most of the smaller ones are hardwood. Softwood is cheaper, so it makes sense to use it for moldings of large cross section. And softwood is not as easy to machine nor does it produce such clean-cut shapes as hardwood on small moldings. You won't get a choice of species, though, so don't try to find moldings to match the hardwood you've used, unless you've been using ramin, the most popular choice for moldings of this type.

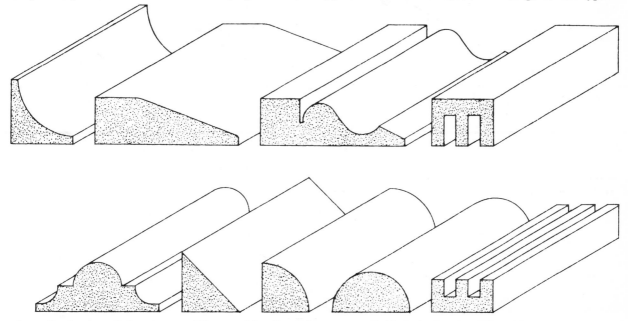

A small selection of the many moldings and beadings that are available in both softwood and hardwood from most woodyards

Floorings and claddings

Two special cross sections are available for use as floorboards and wall paneling, either interior or exterior. Floorboards are softwood planks that have been given a tongue on one edge and a groove on the other, so that they can be interlocked when they are laid. This isn't intended to make them difficult to pry up again. It ensures that when the boards shrink, as they surely will, there will be no unsightly and drafty gaps between the boards. Wall paneling is tongued-and-grooved for the same reason. In addition, the front face is often machined to make it more attractive. Three common profiles are V-jointed and scalloped, intended to be used with the boards vertical, and shiplap, meant to be used with the boards horizontal.

Dowel sections

Round wood sections, called dowels, are produced in both softwood and hardwood. As with elaborate moldings, softwood is used for dowels over 1 in. (25mm) in diameter, and hardwood is used for smaller cross sections, usually from $\frac{1}{4}$ in. (6mm) up to $\frac{3}{4}$ in. (18mm). Dowels have obvious uses for everything from chair rails to playpens and are also used as a means of joining wood together with what are called dowel joints.

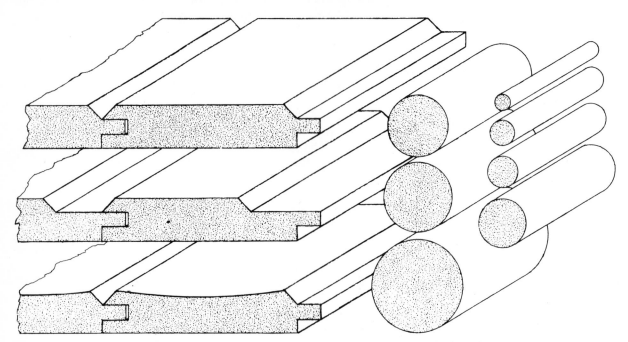

Tongued-and-grooved claddings may have grooves or scallops machined into the board face. Dowel sections (right) come in a wide range of sizes; hardwood is used for some, softwood for others

Man-made sheet materials

One of the biggest drawbacks of wood, as a natural material, is that you cannot have a piece longer than a tree is high, nor thicker than its trunk is wide. Even with a thick trunk only a few wide boards can be cut from the center. The others get progressively narrower as the saw moves toward the outside edge of the log. And with wide boards there is the problem of warping and splitting as well as natural defects in the wood. Man-made sheet materials eliminate all these problems.

Thinking back over the development of woodworking, it is surprising that sheet materials were not produced earlier. The germ of the idea was there all the time, in the use of veneers. The ancient Egyptians knew about veneering, and by the late seventeenth century it was a widespread practice. But the idea of gluing several layers of thin veneer together to make a board was first used on a commercial scale in the nineteenth century, to make tea chests for the China tea trade, and for curved seats on train platforms. This was the first plywood.

But simply gluing thin veneers of wood together isn't the whole story. If you look at a sheet of plywood, you will see that alternate layers have the grain of the veneer at right angles. Two layers stuck together in this way will pull each other into a warped shape, so a third layer is added to stabilize the construction. Further layers make the board even more stable, and of course increase its strength. The end product is a board which is equally strong both with and across the grain and which neither warps, splits nor shrinks. Its size is limited by the size of a sheet of veneer, which is produced by setting a blade against a rotating log to shave off a continuous layer. Veneer sheets can be extremely large.

Blockboard and laminboard are of similar construction. Each has a core of wooden strips, usually of softwood, running edge to edge across the board. This core is then sandwiched between two or more sheets of veneer, whose grain direction is at right angles to that of the core strips. Once again, the board is stable, very strong, and available in large sizes.

The third type of man-made sheet is quite different. It is not made of solid wood at all, but of wood that has been broken down into fibers and reconstituted into a board in the same sort of way as paper is made from wood pulp. It's called hardboard. A variation on hardboard using not wood fibers, but wood chips ground up, mixed with special resins and adhesives and pressed out into a uniform sheet is called particle board or chipboard.

Plywood

Since the basic principle of plywood construction is to stick several thin layers of veneer together with their grain directions opposed in adjacent layers, it is possible to produce a board that is flat, stable and extremely strong. The method of producing the veneers by cutting from a rotating log has the effect, however, of producing a very plain and uninteresting grain pattern in the veneer. The best quality wood used for ordinary plywood is birch, which is a pale-colored wood. Other veneers commonly available include gaboon, beech, mahogany, redwood and pine. You can also buy plywood for decorative use with outer faces of more exotic wood. These veneers are usually sliced across the log to produce the more attractive grain patterns associated with wood cut in this way. Because of the extra expense of using veneers of this type, faced plywoods sometimes have the fine-quality hardwood veneer on only one side, with a less expensive veneer on the other side.

Apart from choosing the surface veneer you want, you can also specify what type of adhesive has been used to make the plywood. There are three types: interior, moisture-resistant and exterior.

Plywood made for interior use, on furniture, wall paneling and the like, will not tolerate damp conditions, so for work that may occasionally get wet you should ask for plywood with moisture-resistant gluing. For outdoor use,

ask for Exterior WBP plywood. This type is extremely durable, but it is only the adhesive that is weatherproof, not the veneers, so the board will not last long unless it is given some form of protective finish like paint or varnish.

Plywood is graded by code letters, which describe the quality of the face veneers. The usual classifications are:

A The best face of the board has a uniform color, is unjointed and free from all defects. This grade is rare and expensive.

B The best face may have variable color, but is clear. The back may be jointed. It is the best grade of plywood generally available.

B/BB Both sides have variable color, and the face side will have some small knots. This is another commonly stocked grade.

BB Both sides of the board have joints and plugged knots.

C One face described as of C quality will have some open defects, usually on the reverse of B or BB graded board.

WG The poorest quality, both faces of the board have splits and other defects. The only guarantee is that the board is well-glued, hence WG.

The grade you choose depends on how you will be using the plywood. If you want to use the plywood in a natural finish, buy the B/BB grade or better. For boards that will be painted, BB or BB/C grades are adequate. If the board will be hidden from view, as the back of a cabinet or the bottom of a

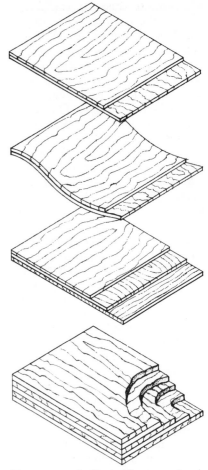

Two opposed plies will warp, three or five are more stable

drawer, grade C will be adequate.

A wide range of thicknesses is available, from $\frac{1}{8}$ in. (3mm) up to 1 in. (25mm). The commonest are $\frac{1}{4}$ in. (6mm), $\frac{3}{8}$ in. (9mm), $\frac{1}{2}$ in. (12mm), $\frac{5}{8}$ in. (15mm), $\frac{3}{4}$ in. (18mm) and 1 in. (25mm).

Blockboard and laminboard

There is one drawback with plywood, at least as far as the thicker boards are concerned. Because of the number of plies that have to be glued together to make up the required thickness, there is a high proportion of adhesive in the plywood, and this makes the sheet hard to work with tools. The way around this is to manufacture a sheet with a solid core, and sandwich it between outer veneer layers. The inner core strips are made of softwood, and are usually glued together side by side. The strips are cut to random lengths which are butt-jointed end to end, although there is sometimes a small gap between lengths. They always run parallel with the long side of the board. The outer veneers are usually hardwood, available in the same species used to make hardwood-faced plywood. There may be one or two veneers on each side of the board but their grain direction is always at right angles to that of the core strips, to counteract any tendency the board may have to warp. In single-veneered boards the outer veneers are slightly thicker than those used for double-faced boards, but even so they often do not mask the inner core construction entirely, and you can often feel a slight ripple running across the face of the board. If you want a perfectly flat surface, buy double-faced boards.

The difference between blockboard and laminboard is in the size of the core strips. The best quality, laminboard, has core strips about $\frac{3}{8}$ in. (9mm) wide, glued together with their grains alternated. Because of the narrowness of the core strips, surface rippling is not noticeable, however laminboard is slightly weaker than blockboard across its width.

Blockboard has core strips about 1 in. (25mm) wide, which makes it somewhat stronger than laminboard, but it is rarely made to such a high quality.

Like plywood, these boards are available with a range of plain surface veneers. The commonest is again birch, and gaboon and mahogany are widely used. You can also buy them with a decorative veneer on one or both sides—teak, oak, sapele and afrormosia are the commonest. Those with one fine veneered surface are used for paneling on cabinets and the like, where only one face of the board will be visible, while the more expensive boards veneered on both sides are used mainly for doors. Unlike plywood, however, blockboard and laminboard are not suitable for outdoor use.

Surface veneers are graded in the same way as for plywood. BB quality is the commonest. Since the sheets will usually be painted, except for the fine-veneered ones, a BB quality will be satisfactory.

Thicknesses of these sheets start at $\frac{1}{2}$ in. (12mm) and go up in steps of $\frac{1}{8}$ in. (3mm) to a thickness of 1 in. (25mm). Thicker sheets, up to $1\frac{3}{4}$ in. (45mm), are usually used only for doors.

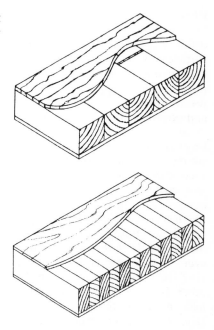

Blockboard (above) has wider core strips than laminboard (below)

Particle board

Particle board, or chipboard, was a brilliant idea for both the woodworker and the manufacturer. For the former, it provides an inexpensive sheet material that can be used for many purposes and for the manufacturer it offers a chance to use up leftovers from sawmills that formerly went to waste. It's a very simple process. Wood chips are ground down to a roughly uniform size, mixed with special resins, and hot-pressed together into a sheet that has no grain direction and so is equally strong and stable in both directions. It is very heavy, however, doesn't take screws and nails very well, and is weaker than the other sheet materials because it has lost the strength that the fiber structure of natural wood gives. It is also fairly hard to work because of the high resin content and tends to blunt tools very quickly.

Raw chipboard has a distinctly granular surface which can look very attractive when stained or painted. Alternatively, it can be treated with a grain filler to give it a perfectly smooth surface, or it can be bought with a surface specially primed and ready for painting. However, it is more widely used as a cheap core material which can be veneered in the same way as plywood and blockboard, using hardwoods cut to reveal the most attractive grain patterns. Or it can be covered with a hardwearing plastic surface that is easy to keep clean. Both veneered and plastic-coated chipboard are widely used both in the furniture industry and by the home woodworker for making a wide range of paneled furniture.

Chipboard is not sold by grades, as are the other man-made sheets. The only variable is the density of the board, which is usually higher for the thinner boards in order to improve their strength, and also for boards intended to be used as flooring. There are moisture-resistant types which can be used out of doors, but generally speaking chipboard should be used only for interior work.

Thicknesses of chipboard usually start at $\frac{1}{4}$ in. (6mm), and go up to 1 in. (25mm). The commonest thicknesses are $\frac{1}{2}$ in. (12mm), $\frac{3}{4}$ in. (18mm) and 1 in. (25mm). Veneered and plastic laminate covered boards are usually available between $\frac{5}{8}$ in. and $\frac{3}{4}$ in. (15 to 18mm) thick, being based on $\frac{5}{8}$ in. (15mm) thick board.

Flaxboard is a similar product to chipboard, but is made from chemically treated flax "shives," the residue of the flax plant after its linen fibers have been removed. These are mixed with resins and then hot-pressed into sheets in the same way as chipboard. The end product is lighter than chipboard, and is made in sizes, from $\frac{1}{2}$ in. (12mm) upwards. It's not widely available.

Particle board comes in various thicknesses, and may be veneered, plastic-coated or tongued-and-grooved along its edges

24

Hardboard

Hardboard is one of the most useful sheet materials for cheap frame and panel work, but is too weak to be used on its own. It is made from pine logs which are chipped up in a similar way to wood pulp in papermaking before being pressed into sheets. Resins are used as binders, but the end product is much softer and easier to work than chipboard, more like a very thick cardboard. Hardboard ranges in color from dark to mid-brown. One side of the board is smooth and slightly shiny, the other has a raised mesh pattern. It bends easily, but because it has soft edges and relatively little strength, it is always used as a cladding on a solid framework, the uprights of which must be fairly close together to prevent the surface of the board from buckling. The surface can be varnished, painted or left plain. Alternatively you can buy hardboard with a surface that has been embossed or perforated with holes, for use as pegboard or with cutouts of various shapes for decorative grilles and so on.

Hardboard is sold in three basic grades, standard, medium and tempered. Standard boards are the cheapest and the most widely available. Medium boards are denser and more resistant to moisture, though both these boards should be confined to indoor use. The toughest and most hardwearing grade, suitable for use out of doors when protected by paint or varnish, and also used for flooring, is oil-tempered hardboard.

The one peculiarity with hardboard, compared with other sheet materials, is the need to condition it before use. The object of this is to equalize the moisture content of the board with its surroundings, without this preparation the board would warp quite severely. To do this, scrub or spray the rough side of the hardboard with clean cold water, and then stack the sheets up on top of each other with rough sides together in pairs. The top sheet should be smooth face upward so that the water doesn't evaporate from the board too quickly. Leave the stack of boards for about 24 hours, or 48 hours if you're using oil-tempered boards. Fix them as soon as possible to their frameworks. If you let them dry out, you will have to go through the conditioning process all over again.

Thicknesses for hardboard range from $\frac{1}{8}$ in. (3mm) upward. Standard and oil-tempered boards come in $\frac{3}{16}$ in. (5mm) and $\frac{1}{4}$ in. (6mm) thicknesses too, while medium boards are usually only sold in $\frac{1}{4}$ in. (6mm), $\frac{3}{8}$ in. (9mm) and $\frac{1}{2}$ in. (12mm) sizes.

Fiberboard is a similar type of material to hardboard, but is much softer and is sold in thicker sheets—commonly $\frac{1}{2}$ in. (12mm) and $\frac{3}{4}$ in. (18mm) thicknesses. It's useful for pinboards.

Sheet sizes

The commonest size of sheet for all the man-made materials is the 4 ×

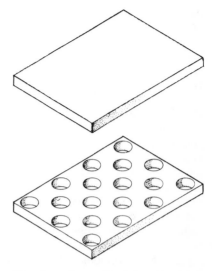

Hardboard, usually $\frac{1}{8}$ in. (3mm) thick, may be plain or perforated

8 ft. sheet, (1220 × 2440mm). In addition to this, you will find a wide variety of other sizes, both square and rectangular, which may suit the work you're planning better than the standard 4 × 8 ft. sheet—either because you can cut certain shapes out more easily, or because wastage will be kept to a minimum.

CHAPTER 2
The timber supply industry

Many industrialized countries have exhausted their stocks of native wood. Britain, once a heavily-forested island, now has less than one tenth of its land area covered by trees, and many other countries have been similarly stripped of their forests. These countries import their wood from countries whose stocks are larger. However, they too will soon run down their stocks unless trees are treated as a crop instead of as a raw material. This view is the foundation of the forestry and wood industry of today; planting, harvesting and replanting of trees to ensure a continuous supply for future generations.

The cycle of the industry is quite straightforward. The trees are felled, stripped of most of their superficial growth, and then transported to the sawmill, either in the country of origin or the country that's importing the wood. There it is sawn into more manageable sections, ready for the most vital part of its preparation: seasoning.

When a tree is felled it contains up to twice its own weight in water. If the wood is used in this state it will shrink considerably, and will also split or warp. Seasoning is a carefully controlled process that dries out most of this moisture, increasing the strength of the wood and also making it easier to work. There are two methods of doing this, air drying and kiln drying.

Air drying means stacking the sawn wood in such a way that air can circulate around the boards and evaporate the moisture. The boards are arranged in a large stack, built up on low piers with each layer of boards separated from the next by small strips of wood. The stack is covered to protect the wood from the effects of the weather, heavy rain and hot sun, in particular.

Softwoods dry out fairly quickly because of their relatively open grain structure, and so are usually stacked in the spring.

Boards an inch (25mm) thick will dry to 20 per cent moisture content in two to three months. Hardwoods are more closely grained and so dry out more slowly. They are usually stacked in autumn or winter, when the cold damp weather will allow the drying out to proceed more slowly at first. Hardwood boards an inch (25mm) thick, stacked in the autumn, will be down to 20 per cent moisture by the following summer. If the wood is going to be used in a heated house, its moisture content will have to be lowered further to 10 or 12 per cent to ensure that it will not shrink or warp.

A quicker and more controllable method of seasoning, used increasingly nowadays, is kiln drying. This is done in a closed compartment in which the air circulation and rate of drying can be regulated exactly to produce wood of a specific moisture content, lower than that produced by air drying, an advantage if the wood is to be used immediately. The wood is stacked in the same way as for air drying, but in smaller piles that can be wheeled into the kiln. Another advantage of kiln drying is that wood-destroying fungi and wood-boring insects are usually killed off by the process. However, this will not prevent them from attacking the wood again, and so the next stage in the process is to treat the wood with preservatives. Hardwoods are usually fairly resistant to insect and fungal attack, but softwood is not. Since so much is used in house construction, it makes sense to try to make it last as long as possible. Preservatives are forced into the wood by pressure and vacuum techniques which ensure that deep penetration is achieved. This doesn't mean you cannot paint or varnish the wood though it may give the bare wood a characteristic green tinge.

The wood is now ready for its final machining. Larger boards are cut down into smaller sections, planed or machined into whatever shape may be needed, and dispatched from the sawmill to the lumberyard. Here the wood must again be properly stored, preferably under cover, until it is sold, either directly to the user, or to retailers who keep only a small stock and rely on larger lumberyards for regular supplies.

Sawmills operate on a truly heroic scale, cutting vast logs down to more manageable proportions

Buying wood

Now that you know something about the types of wood you can buy, how they are cut, graded and sold, you're ready to go shopping for the raw material. How much you should remember, and how seriously you need to apply your knowledge, depends on the sort of woodworker you want to be. The person who is making a bookshelf or a simple box isn't going to worry a lot about the wood, as long as it's about the right size. But someone who is going to cut, shape and finish the wood into a piece of fine furniture will want to know every detail about the wood before buying it. Here are the most important points to remember in making sure the wood you get is the wood you want to use.

Species

Softwood is generally available and will be sold by color more often than by species. Hardwood is sold only by some specialist suppliers, and may have to be ordered in advance. Many suppliers have sample pieces which you can use to compare color and grain pattern, and which may help you to find a suitable substitute if you can't get exactly the species you want.

Surface

You can buy wood rough sawn or planed all around, often abbreviated to PAR or, in America, S4S, meaning surfaced on four sides. Sawn wood is naturally cheaper than planed wood of the same size, and unless you are intending to use a stock size, you will save money by buying the next largest stock size in sawn wood and doing the finishing yourself.

Quality

Large lumberyards stock a wide range of qualities in softwood, and perhaps one or two grades of hardwood too. Specify which you want, and make sure you get it.

Dimensions

Remember that quoted dimensions are nominal, not actual. Sawn wood is fractionally smaller than the nominal size, while planed boards will have lost at least $\frac{1}{8}$ in. (3mm) on each dimension, and probably more on larger sizes. If you want exactly a certain size board, you will have to buy the next largest stock size and plane it down to the size you want yourself. On length, order either standard lengths, and check them, or buy by the foot.

Buying sheet material

The same criteria apply to buying board materials as for wood. A small scale woodworker will not worry too much, as long as the board is the right thickness and it takes the required finish. But for the discriminating woodworker, there are a lot of points to remember.

Sheet type

The first factor is the type of sheet. You will probably want plywood for thinner cladding on furniture, and for compartments, shelves and small scale panel constructions. Blockboard and laminboard are ideal for unsupported panels—desk and table tops, for example. Chipboard is used to make utility furniture without a framework, hardboard requires a framework.

Surface/veneer

If you are planning to stain or varnish your work, you will want a surface that is either first quality, or is specially veneered with hardwood for decorative purposes. If you are going to paint it, the standard need not be so high, and if the board surface will be hidden or seldom seen, then you can take advantage of the cheaper price of a lower-quality board.

Dimensions

Choose the board thickness to suit the application. A load-bearing surface will obviously have to be thicker than a purely decorative surface.

Costing your wood

When you go shopping for wood, there's one vital factor to take into consideration: how much it is going to cost. In most cases the price is as important as all the other factors involved.

Softwood is usually priced by the linear foot, or by the meter, according to its cross section.

In America, a unit called the board foot is used for most wood sizes. This is the amount of wood in a piece 1 in. thick, 1 ft. wide and 1 ft. long. So a board 1 in. thick, 6 in. wide and 6 ft. long will contain $1 \times \frac{1}{2} \times 6 = 3$ board feet, and so on. Hardwood may be priced by the linear foot, or for larger cross sections, by volume in a unit called a cube or cubic foot.

Boards are priced by the square foot or by the square meter. The former is fairly easy to reckon up, since most boards are cut to "whole foot" sizes, while the latter is difficult to work out from the sheet size without a calculator. It is usually easier to ask for a sheet price, and let whoever is selling you the wood do the sums.

When you have worked out the quantities required in each material, the next job is to get quotations from several different suppliers. If the order is a relatively simple one, you can probably ask for prices over the telephone. But for more complex orders, it is better to write everything down and take the list into the supplier for him to cost up item by item. A little time spent doing this could result in substantial savings on your final bill.

Generally speaking, large yards will be cheaper than smaller outlets selling only a restricted range. But you may have to take your place in line behind trade customers with bigger orders than yours. For this reason it is a good idea to plan your buying well in advance. This will also leave time for you to finish the seasoning of the wood you buy by storing it at home in the room where it will be used.

Ask for discounts if you are buying large amounts of wood of a particular type, or if your total order is large.

Inspection

When you are buying wood and sheet materials, you must remember that however carefully you specify exactly what you want at the lumberyard, you may not get exactly that. Because wood is a natural product, a grading system cannot be rigorously applied since every piece is slightly different from the one next to it.

The greatest key to success is careful inspection of every piece of wood and sheet that you buy. This will ensure that your wood is the species and quality you want, and that its appearance is what you expected—the right color, grain pattern and knottiness, if these factors are of importance for the job you are doing. It also means that you will have a chance to spot defects in the wood that could weaken it structurally or mar its appearance, and to reject pieces that have inherent faults or that have been damaged by careless handling in the yard. Check that lengths of softwood are not warped by looking along their length. Examine the cut ends for splits, bowing and other damage. Check both faces of sheet materials for quality and see that they are free of marks and knocks; also look closely at corners and edges for signs of damage. On veneered boards parts of the veneer may be lifted or split and may have been badly repaired.

Watch out for errors in making up your order, specify wood of the right quality, species and dimension. It's easy to correct errors while you are still at the suppliers but much more difficult to do it once you've taken the wood home.

Matching existing woodwork

If you are buying new wood in order to match an existing piece of work, there is only one foolproof way of doing it well, and that is to compare the existing piece with the new wood side by side. If you cannot take the piece you are trying to match to the yard, ask if you can take some wood samples home for comparison purposes, and use the best-matching sample to select the wood you want from the stocks at the yard.

Getting wood home

Most suppliers will deliver large quantities of wood and sheet material, but in some cases you will want to transport it home yourself as soon as you have bought it. If you have a roofrack on your car, there will be no problem, as long as you tie the wood on securely and make sure it is protected where it comes in contact with the rack. Make sure particularly that the fronts of large sheets are tied down securely. As you drive along the air flow over the car can lift and break all but the thicker boards.

A station wagon or a hatchback model is also an ideal way of carrying wood, as long as the rear door is tied down if it has to be left open.

If you have neither roofrack nor station wagon, all you can do is pass long pieces of wood into the car through the rear window into the front passenger's foot space. This is the only method that does not interfere with the driver's control of the car. Make sure you protect the wood where it rests on the window frame, and tie it to door handles or armrests if necessary. This won't work with large boards or sheets, of course.

Once you've bought your wood and transported it home you need somewhere to store it.

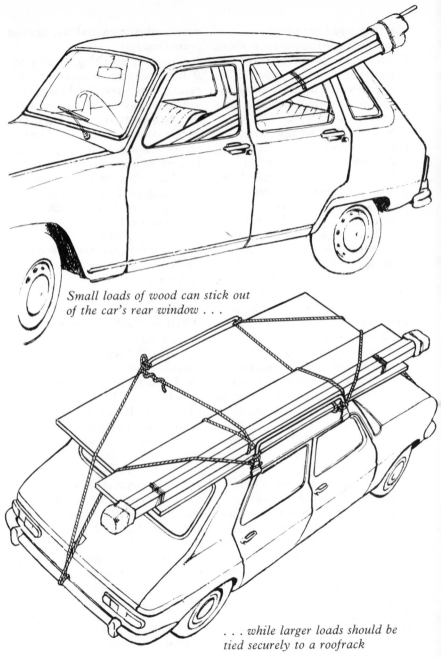

Small loads of wood can stick out of the car's rear window . . .

. . . while larger loads should be tied securely to a roofrack

30

Storing wood at home

You must store the wood carefully if you are not going to use it immediately. For long term storage, it should be kept somewhere cool but dry, in a garage or attic, for example. The best way of storing it is in some form of stack, like the stacks used for the drying of boards when they are naturally seasoned. In an attic, lay the wood across the ceiling joists, using small spacers to separate each layer from the one above it. In a garage, construct a ceiling rack from sawn wood and suspend it from the roof. Move the spacers slightly from time to time to prevent any risk of the face of the wood being marked. If neither of these methods are possible, another way to store wood and prevent it from warping is to stand it upright in some sort of floor rack. This method won't stop the boards from curling across the width, and if they are leaning in the rack instead of being upright, they will take on a permanent sag.

Sheets are not easy to store flat in this way because of their width. The best way of storing them is vertically, either standing against a wall with some sort of restraint to keep them there, or better still on a wall rack, constructed perhaps from shelving brackets tilted upward at a slight angle to hold the sheets back against the wall behind. Be careful to protect the edges and corners of the sheets from being damaged.

Shortly before you use any of your wood stock for any con-struction within the house, bring it into the room where it will be used and stack it for a few days so its moisture content can drop to that of its surroundings. This will lessen still further the risk of any shrinkage or warping taking place. Board materials, except hard-board, do not need conditioning.

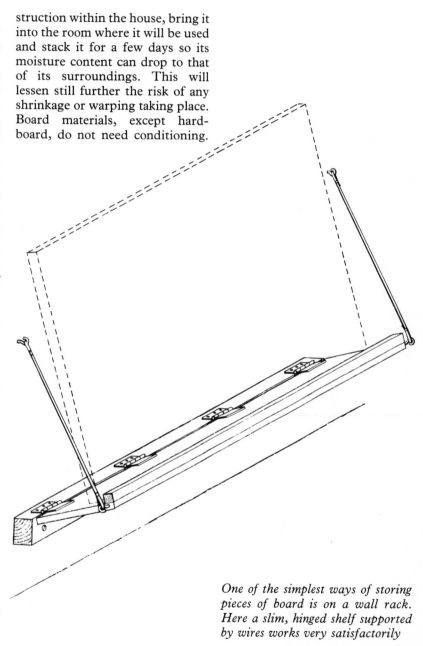

One of the simplest ways of storing pieces of board is on a wall rack. Here a slim, hinged shelf supported by wires works very satisfactorily

31

CHAPTER 3
Tools for a purpose

The evolution of hand tools from the most primitive stone ax to the sophisticated tools of today parallels the growth of civilization. We have learned almost all we know of primitive man from the tools he left behind, and later civilizations have bequeathed us such a store of tools that we can trace the ancestry of all the woodworking tools we use today back through the centuries. Behind each is the need to design a tool for a purpose.

Take hammering, for example. We think immediately of driving nails, but to begin with the hammer was a tool for chipping out a cutting edge from a raw flint. Adding a handle was the big breakthrough, enabling the user to direct his blows with increased precision and force. By the time the Romans turned their ingenuity to the hammer, they had produced the nail to drive with it, and had also made its head in iron with a claw for pulling out the nails they bent.

The saw shows similar development. Copper provided the material for the first toothed saw, an Egyptian model from about 1500 BC which worked on the pull stroke, not the push stroke like today's saws. The reason was quite simple; the soft blade simply buckled if it was pushed through the wood. The Romans added a few improvements to the saw, notably setting the teeth to one side and the other to lessen the friction of cutting, and the use of files and saw sets to keep the teeth in good condition. It was not until the

seventeenth century that rolling mills could produce broad strips of steel from which a saw cutting on the push stroke could be made.

Frame saws, those with a thin blade held taut in a handle, underwent a parallel development, and by the sixteenth century their blades were being made of the finest clock-spring steel, strong and fine enough for even the most intricate work.

Boring holes was a trickier task. To begin with, a rotating bit simply ground out a hole by the use of an abrasive paste such as quartz sand. It developed into an auger resembling a half pipe with a sharpened end, and this gave way to the spiral-threaded auger in the early Middle Ages which was at first turned by hand. The wooden brace appeared around 1400, with a square hole in its simple chuck to hold a square-ended bit. The introduction of the iron brace, first noted in 1505, increased its boring capacity dramatically. The hand drill was later in developing. The earliest geared model dates from about 1800, and it was not until the mid-nineteenth century that machine-made gears became widely available, and the drill we know today appeared.

Chisels evolved early as cutting tools for wood and stone; the skill of the Egyptians in making elaborately jointed furniture testifies to that. First copper, hardened by hammering, gave a cutting edge of some durability; then bronze, cast with a pointed tang on to which a

handle could be fitted, and later iron, forged and hardened, led to the chisel we know today.

The plane, however, is an oddity that seems to have sprung from nowhere. It is unique in the way it shaves wood to a carefully controlled depth, and seems to have been yet another Roman invention. No tool has been found earlier than an iron plane from Pompeii that looks like a bench plane of today.

Measuring and marking tools for checking distance, squareness and trueness, both horizontal and vertical, date from Egyptian times. The folding rule was another Roman idea, but the Egyptians can claim the square and the plumb bob. The spirit level in its present form dates from around 1660.

Last, but by no means least, comes the screw and the screwdriver to turn it. Metal screws appeared around the mid-fifteenth century, when they were handmade and square-headed like bolts and were turned by a sort of box wrench that a car mechanic would recognize.

Slotted-head screws followed later, with the first use of a screwdriver being noted in 1744 in a brace fitted with a screwdriver bit. The screwdriver first appeared around 1800, and once screws could be mass-produced instead of being laboriously hand-cut, its future was assured.

Now that you know just how long most of our familiar tools have been around, let's consider them according to their purpose.

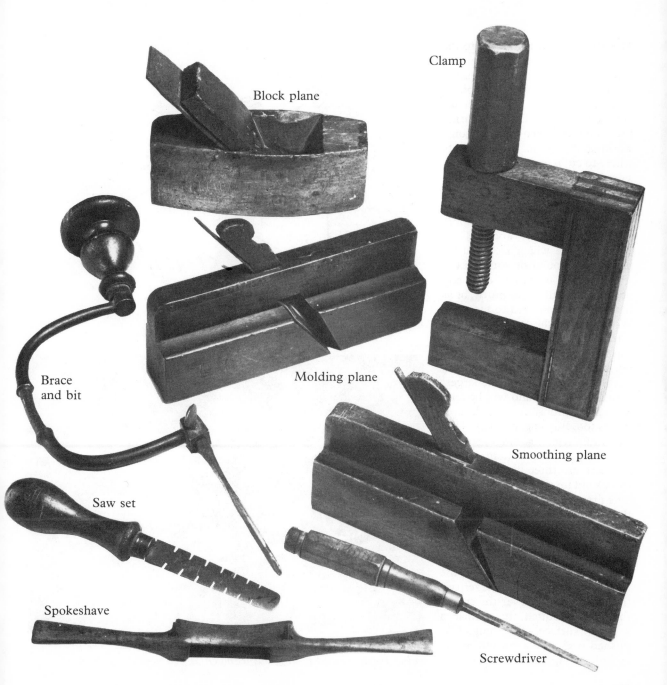

Block plane

Clamp

Brace and bit

Molding plane

Smoothing plane

Saw set

Spokeshave

Screwdriver

Measuring and marking tools

Unless you are a woodworking genius with the carpenter's equivalent of the musician's perfect pitch, you will not be able to make anything without first measuring the wood and then making some working marks on it to indicate where to cut it and join it together. For this you need five basic tools.

Steel tape

The first is a steel measuring tape, a thin strip of steel about $\frac{5}{8}$ in. (15mm) wide which is coiled up neatly in a round or square case. The free end is marked zero, and you simply pull out as much, or as little tape as you need to measure. When you let the end go, a spring retracts the tape into the case. You can buy these tapes in a variety of lengths; a 10 ft. (3m) long one will enable you to measure the largest boards with ease, and will be long enough for most room measurements too. Buy one with both inch and millimeter markings, so that you can use either system.

There are three useful features to look out for when you buy a tape. The first is a retractable tongue on the end of the rule, which is designed to enable both internal and external measurements to be taken with equal accuracy. Hooked over the end of a piece of wood, the tongue pulls out so that the zero on the tape is exactly over the end of the wood. Butted up against a vertical surface, the tongue is pushed back into a cut-out in the end of the tape, so that the end of

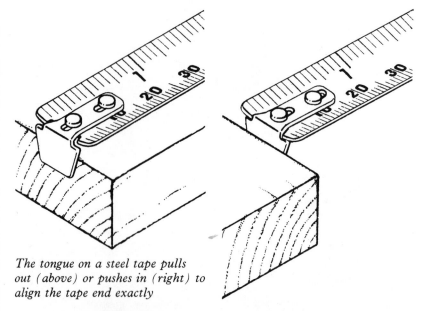

The tongue on a steel tape pulls out (above) or pushes in (right) to align the tape end exactly

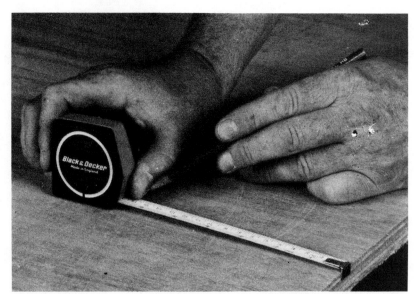

Use a steel tape to measure lengths by hooking the tongue over the end of the wood and pulling out as much as you need

34

the tape is in line with the surface from which you are measuring.

Next on the list of features is a lock, which enables you to keep a length of tape extended from the case without the spring retracting it. The third is a choice of markings on the tape itself: black on white or black on yellow are the most common. Pick the easiest to read.

Treat the tape with care so that it remains accurate. Don't drop it, and don't leave it with the tape locked in an extended position. If you kink or crush it, it will no longer retract correctly and will be almost useless for accurate work, since it will not lie flat. Clean the whole length of the tape from time to time, wiping it over with a cloth dipped in light oil.

Squares

The second basic tool you need is a square. Use this to mark lines for saw cuts or joints exactly at right angles to the face or edge of the wood you're working on, and to test that edges, frames and boxes are perfectly square after preparation or assembly. Choose either a try square or a combination square.

The try square usually has a steel blade and a wooden or plastic stock. Place the stock against the face or edge of the wood, with your thumb pressing the face of the stock, the first two fingers holding the blade and the remaining fingers resting on the wood surface. Then you can mark a line at right angles to the stock against either side of the blade, using a pencil for rough

work or a marking knife for finer work. A cut line is not only thinner than a pencil line, it cuts across the grain of the wood which might deflect a pencil point and it provides a locating mark for edge tools such as chisels and saws. It also helps to prevent the wood fibers from splitting at each side of the cut during sawing, which is frequently a problem on boards with thin surface veneers.

You can buy special marking knives, but for most general work an all-purpose trimming knife will do. Or use a penknife, which is less bulky to carry around in a pocket or work apron.

The try square has another vital function. It can be used to test the

Use a try square with the stock pressed firmly against the edge of the wood and the fingers pressing down on the blade

35

flatness of surfaces, by laying the outer edge of the blade across the surface. If you can find one with inches or millimeters engraved on the blade, you can use it for setting gauges and for dividing wood into equal sections that can't be worked out easily using arithmetic (page 134). One with a blade 6 in. (150mm) long will be adequate for most work.

The combination square is frowned on by the perfectionist woodworker, yet it's a multi-purpose tool that can be very useful to the handyman. Its stock is adjustable, sliding up and down a metal blade to which it can be locked by means of a small wheel. You use it as you would a try square for testing squareness and flatness. You can also check a recess for squareness by setting the stock in from the end of the blade by a distance slightly less than the recess width.

In addition to this, the sliding stock has a second edge at 45° to the blade, so you can use it for marking miters accurately.

It is most important that you take good care of a square. Don't drop it, keep it free of rust by wiping the blade occasionally with petroleum jelly, and rub wooden stocks with a little linseed oil. Check that it *is* square from time to time by the simple test of placing the square against a straight edge and marking a line on the surface below with your marking knife. Then reverse the square and make another line. The marks should coincide if the square is accurate.

Marking gauge

You will find it hard to do without a marking gauge. It is used for marking a line exactly parallel to the edge of a piece of wood, whether along the grain or on end grain. It has four parts: the stem, stock, thumbscrew and spur. The stock slides along the stem and can be locked to it at any distance from the spur by means of the thumb-screw. The face of the stock is then placed against the edge of the wood, with the spur resting on the face to be marked and pointing in the opposite direction to that in which the gauge will be moved. The stock is then pushed along the edge of the wood, drawing the spur after it. Press firmly, but not too hard. If you press hard the point may follow the grain pattern, not the line you want to mark.

Set the distance from stock to spur by holding the gauge along-side the tape, or the edge of a square if it has measurements. Check it by marking a line on a piece of scrap wood and measuring the distance from edge to line. If it is accurate, make sure that the thumbscrew is tight and then mark the workpiece.

You can also use a marking gauge to find the exact center of a piece of wood. Set the distance between stock and spur to roughly half the wood's width, and make marks on the wood face with the stock held first against one edge of the wood, then against the other. Adjust the stock position slightly and re-test. When the marks co-

The combination square allows you to mark the wood at 45° angles. A marking knife produces a cleaner line than a pencil

incide you have located the exact center of the width.

As with the wooden stock of the try square, the wooden parts of the marking gauge will benefit from an occasional light rub over with linseed oil. Sand over any nicks to the edges, and keep the point sharp by occasional use of a metal file or an oilstone. If you do happen to bend or break the marking point, you can replace it with a small nail driven through the stem and filed carefully to a sharp, symmetrical point.

Pencil

On many occasions you will need a pencil, though you should use a knife or gauge for marking cutting lines on the wood. Use a pencil for marking the face edge and face side of the workpiece, for hatching in areas that will be cut off as waste, for numbering joints and for marking shapes on the wood. Choose at least an HB pencil, and preferably a softer one, keep it sharp but without too long a point, and store it behind your ear. All *real* carpenters do.

Spirit level

The last in the group of basic measuring and marking tools, the spirit level, actually does neither of these things. Instead it tests that your work is level, a fact that is important mainly for built-in items such as shelves and cupboards on walls and units standing on the floor. It consists of a straight stock with parallel sides in which are set one or more glass or plastic phials filled with fluid and the all-important bubble. The phial's position is set within the stock so that when it is precisely level, the bubble lies exactly between the two marks on the phial. Many spirit levels also incorporate a phial at each end, so that the level can test accurate verticals as well as horizontals. Buy one with a metal stock which is less prone to damage than a wooden stock, and treat it gently. Choose one at least 12 in. (305mm) long, and preferably twice that size for accurate leveling of wall battens and built-in furniture.

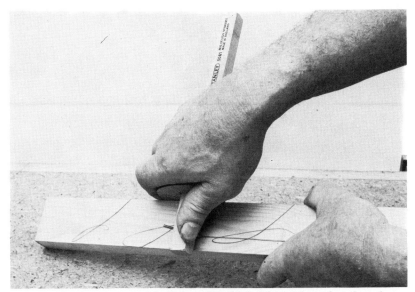

Use the marking gauge with the stock held firmly against the edge of the wood and push it away from you to mark the line

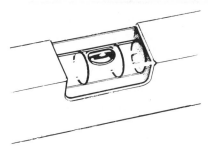

The spirit level indicates true horizontals when the air bubble lies exactly between the two marks on the phial.

Some less common measuring and marking tools

Now for a quick look at some of the measuring and marking tools that are less common.

The mortise gauge is a marking gauge with two pins, used for marking out mortise and tenon joints. Another gauge, the cutting gauge, is similar to the marking gauge but has a small sharpened cutter, held in by a brass wedge, instead of a fixed spur, and is used for marking precision work across the grain.

The sliding bevel is a sort of adjustable square. It is used for marking angles that are not 45° or 90°; you will need a protractor to set it to the required angle. It's not needed often.

The boxwood rule is useful for measuring short lengths, but it's becoming a rather expensive item to buy. You can improvise using a tape measure and the graduated stock of a square, or buy a 12 in. (305mm) steel rule instead; it will be much cheaper.

Compasses and dividers are useful for some marking-out work, and for drawing curves. If you have some school ones around the house, use these; if not, improvise.

Last comes the dovetail template, essential for making dovetail joints but only used for this purpose (page 104).

All these tools, with the exception of the mortise gauge are really needed only by the advanced woodworker, who will use them often enough to justify the cost of adding them to his tool kit.

The mortise gauge is a very useful aid for accurate marking out of mortise and tenon joints

The sliding bevel is an adjustable square used for marking angles of any size

Cutting

Now that you can measure how long your workpiece is going to be, and you have marked one end square and the other end the correct distance away, you have to cut it to length. How long the cut is and which direction it takes through the wood will determine the type of saw you use. There are three types to choose from: the hand saw, the back saw and the frame saw.

Hand saws

The hand saw is used for heavy cutting jobs like ripping boards to narrower widths and for cutting across thick sections of wood. There are two types of hand saw, the ripsaw and the crosscut saw. The difference between them is the way they are made, either to rip wood, that is cut along the grain, or crosscut, cut across the grain.

The wood fibers are aligned along the grain, and the best way of cutting the wood in this direction is to slice it away like a chisel. The teeth of a ripsaw are each sharpened like a chisel, and are set with their cutting edges at right angles to the blade. Alternate teeth are splayed slightly to one side and the other to make the saw cut a little wider than the blade. This stops the blade from sticking in the cut.

In contrast, the crosscut saw has to cut across the fibers of the wood instead of chiseling them away in the direction in which they lie. So the teeth of a crosscut saw are sharpened like tiny knives. The teeth are again set alternately to one side of the blade and the other, but the action of the saw is to make two parallel cuts across the wood a short distance apart. The cut fibers in between crumble away as sawdust. The cutting edges of the teeth are set at about 70° to the blade, instead of 90° as with the ripsaw.

The other important points of difference between rip and crosscut saws are in blade length and in the number of teeth per inch (25mm) of saw blade. A ripsaw is usually around 26 in. (660mm) long, and has about five tooth points to the inch (25mm), while the crosscut saw is about 22 in. (560mm) long and has about 10 tooth points per inch (25mm).

The panel saw is just a crosscut saw with somewhat smaller teeth, and got its name from its traditional use in cutting up panels for furniture backs and drawer bottoms, where a coarser saw would have splintered the relatively thin wood. It will cut wood along the grain slowly, but since most of your work will be crosscutting and panel work, this saw will be ideal for general-purpose cutting.

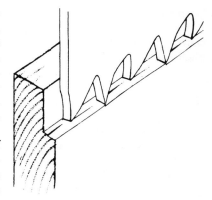

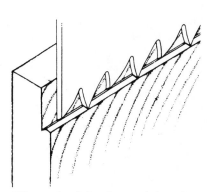

The teeth of the ripsaw (above) are shaped like tiny chisels to slice away the wood. The crosscut saw has knife shaped teeth to cut through the wood fibers

Using a hand saw

Whatever material you are sawing, start the cut by placing the saw blade on the waste side of the cutting line you have marked, with your thumb next to it as a guide. Draw the blade upward for two or three short strokes to start the cut. Then move your hand away a little, using it to hold the wood steady as you saw. Keep the blade at a fairly low angle to the wood for the first few strokes, and use the full length of the blade in a steady down-and-up action. Gradually raise the blade angle until it is about 60° for ripsawing or 45° for crosscutting and continue cutting until you near the other edge of the wood. If you saw straight through there is a risk that the weight of the waste section will cause the board to break off, perhaps splitting your workpiece. To prevent this, support the waste part with your free hand, and complete the cut gently.

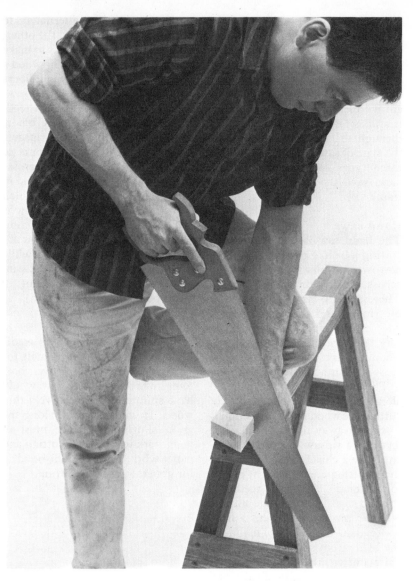

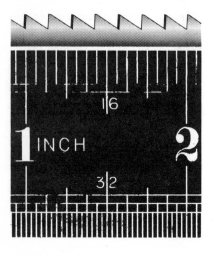

Left: the coarseness of a saw blade is measured by the number of teeth per inch of blade

Above: keep your arm and shoulder in line with the blade, and your eye over the cutting line

40

Cutting across the grain of the wood with the workpiece held firmly against a bench hook (see page 146 for instructions for making a bench hook)

Cutting along the grain, or rip-sawing, with the wood supported between two sawhorses

Back saws

Back saws are so called because the blade of the saw is stiffened with a rib of brass or steel running along the back or top edge. They are used for cutting joints and for other small scale work on wood of relatively small cross section. The most common back saw is the tenon saw, which as its name suggests is used mainly for cutting the tenon or tongue part of mortise and tenon joints. The blade is usually 10 or 12 in. (250 or 305mm) long, and has around 14 teeth per inch (25mm). Note that with this saw, the back of the blade limits the depth of the cut.

Using a tenon saw

Unlike the hand saw, the tenon saw is used in a more or less horizontal position. As it is fairly heavy in relation to its size, little pressure is needed to work with it. Start the cut, and support the waste if necessary, in the same way as with a hand saw, but keep the angle of the blade low throughout the cut.

You can also use the tenon saw for cutting thin sheet materials and plastic laminates, when a finer cut than the hand saw can provide is needed. As before, the angle of the saw cut is kept low.

Frame saws

Because sawing isn't always limited to straight cuts, you need a saw that can cope with curves, and the only sort of blade that can do this is a thin, flexible one. Since using such a blade alone would buckle it

Above: the tenon saw being used to cut out a halving joint. It is the ideal tool for all joint cutting, and also for crosscutting wood of small cross section

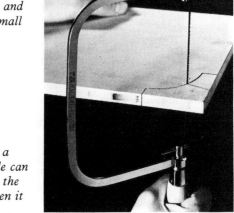

Right: the coping saw cutting a curve in blockboard. The blade can be turned to follow the line of the cut and is simply replaced when it gets blunt

in no time, it is held taut in a frame of wood, or more usually, metal. The coping saw is the most popular frame saw, and will cut most of the curves you will need to make. It has a steel frame, holding a blade about $5\frac{1}{2}$ in. (139mm) long. The blade is usually fitted with its teeth pointing away from the handle so that it cuts on the forward stroke.

Using a coping saw

Obviously you can cut no farther from the edge of your workpiece than the distance between the blade and the frame. For cuts starting at the edge of the wood, begin the cut as you would with a flat-bladed saw. As the cut proceeds, turn the blade in its frame by rotating the pins on which it is held, in order to keep the blade parallel with the intended cutting line and to maintain the maximum distance between blade and frame. Finish the cut by returning to the wood's edge, being careful not to split the surface.

For enclosed cuts, first drill a hole in the workpiece. Then remove the blade from the saw by unscrewing the handle, thread it through the hole in the wood and replace its end in the frame, tightening the handle fully before starting to saw. Make sure you have adequate frame clearance all around, and then reverse the blade threading sequence to disengage the blade when the cut is completed.

Taking care of your saw

A sharp saw is vital if you are going to cut wood cleanly and without undue effort. Try to avoid damaging the teeth; always fit a blade guard as soon as you have finished using the saw, and don't knock the blade against other tools. Keep the blade free of rust, and store your saws by suspending them from the handle. If the teeth do get damaged, try to get them reset and sharpened by an expert—it's a very difficult job to do accurately yourself. However, a little careful touching up of the cutting edges with a small triangular file will help keep your saw in good condition between "services."

The coping saw has replaceable blades which are relatively cheap. When the one in use is blunt or buckled, simply remove it from the frame and fit a new one.

Specialized saws

The dovetail saw is a smaller version of the tenon saw, with a blade about 8 in. (200mm) long and with about 18 teeth per inch (25mm). It is used for cutting dovetail joints (page 110) where a fine cut is essential for accuracy.

Other less common frame saws are the bow saw, used for cutting curves on thick wood, and the fretsaw, a lighter version of the coping saw. A fretsaw has a deeper frame, and is used for intricate cutting on thin sheet materials.

Another saw you may need from time to time is the padsaw, which has a thin flexible blade and is used for cutting holes in thick wood, where a frame saw's blade would break, for example to make keyholes. It can only be started in the wood from a pilot hole drilled in the waste area of the workpiece.

Shaping

With the wood measured, marked and cut to length, you are faced with the next stage in its preparation, shaping it to your exact requirements. This might involve making it thinner, rounding its edges or cutting parts of it away to form joints. The tools you need to carry out these jobs are a plane, some chisels and one or more abrasive tools.

Planes

There are two groups of planes, bench planes and special purpose planes. The bench plane is used for reducing wood in cross section, and for smoothing the surface after sawing. Special purpose planes are used for producing special features such as grooves and moldings. The amateur woodworker has little need for the latter type, but a bench plane is essential. Even if only stock sizes of machine-planed wood are used, the surface will often be neither flat enough nor true enough for accurate work, unless it is planed first.

Bench planes come in several sizes. The smallest, called a smoothing plane, measures about 10 in. (250mm) in length. It is the best choice for a first plane, since it is light enough to handle with ease and will cope with most basic tasks which require a plane. The jack plane which is 15 in. (381mm) long, the fore or trying plane, about 18 in. (457mm) long and the jointer plane, up to 24 in. (610mm) long, are of more use on large-scale

work, where long edges have to be planed exactly flat and true. For such work a short plane would merely follow the undulations of the surface, like a small boat on a choppy sea.

Using a plane

First, make sure the wood you are planing is firmly held on the bench. Then stand with feet comfortably apart and the weight of your shoulders directly over the plane. Keep your elbow well tucked in, and move the plane along the workpiece in one sweep from end to end, shifting your weight from one leg to the other so the plane is moving as part of you. On very long pieces of work you actually walk with the plane along the length of the wood.

Try to start the cut with more pressure on the front handle of the plane than on the back. Ease up as you pass the plane along the work, until at the end the pressure is more on the back end of the plane. If the shavings are thick, try setting the blade in a little. It takes much less effort to remove three thin shavings than one thick one, and the resulting work will be smoother and more accurate.

If you are planing wood down to size, you will already have marked the final thickness you want on the wood, using the marking gauge. Do this on both sides of the wood, and check regularly as you plane to make sure you don't plane off too much. Check that the planed edge is square to the others by using the try square.

For planing wood that is narrower than the plane's sole, guide the plane with your front hand to stop it from wobbling. On wide surfaces, it's often easier to work with the plane held slightly across the grain direction, so that the blade slices through the wood at an angle instead of meeting it head-on. There are times when you want to trim wood to length and there is too little to cut off to use a saw for the job. A plane is the tool to use here. The problem with planing end grain is that as you plane across the wood, it splinters at the far side. There's a simple way to stop this from happening, though. Simply clamp a piece of scrap wood against the workpiece, level with the end you are planing, and plane across the two together. Then any splintering occurs on the far side of the scrap wood, not on your workpiece. Make sure that the blade is sharp when planing end grain, and set it to give a very fine cut so you don't remove too much wood with a stroke.

Taking care of your plane

Planes are precision tools and are fragile. Drop them, and even if they don't break you risk damaging or distorting the plane body or its mechanism, with serious consequences to your workmanship. Always put the plane down on its side, never on its sole. Keep it clean and lightly oiled, and ensure that the blade is kept free of rust. And put it away right after use, preferably in its box with a piece of rust-inhibiting paper.

When planing narrow edges, use your front hand to steady the plane and guide it is so it does not wobble from side to side

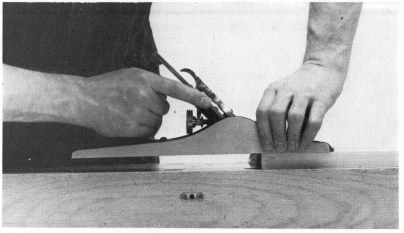

Start planing with more pressure on the front of the plane than on the back. Ease up as you plane along the wood, pressing down on the back as you reach the other end of the wood

Adjusting a plane

The main parts of the plane are indicated on the drawing below. The plane is one tool you have to keep taking apart if you are going to keep it in good condition, so it is important to familiarize yourself with the various parts and their functions, and how they fit together.

To remove the blade, first lift the wedge lever and slide the wedge out. Then you can lift out the top iron and cutter, which you will see are screwed together. Lay them in the angle of the bench hook, *not* in your hand, and loosen the screw with a wide-bladed screwdriver, so that you can turn the iron through 90° and lift off the cutter. When you have resharpened the blade (page 48), screw the iron and cutter together again tightly. Set the edge of the iron about $\frac{1}{16}$ in. (1.5mm) from the edge of the blade, making sure that their two edges are parallel and that there is no gap between them. The blade's bevel must be on the underside.

Put the blade and iron back in place in the mouth of the plane, fit the wedge over them and press down the wedge lever fully. If the assembly is at all loose after this, tighten up the center screw a little. If, on the other hand, the lever won't depress fully, the plane probably isn't put together properly and you'll have to dismantle and reassemble it.

Adjust the depth of the cut the plane makes by turning the knurled wheel in front of the rear handle. This wheel moves the whole cutter assembly up and down. Set the blade out too far, and you won't be able to plane at all because the blade will tear up the wood; not far enough, and it will barely cut at all.

In addition to this adjustment, you must also make sure that the blade edge is exactly parallel with the sole. If not, it will cut deeper at one side than the other. To check it, hold the plane sole uppermost and look along the sole, aligning the blade by moving the adjusting lever. Now your plane is ready to use.

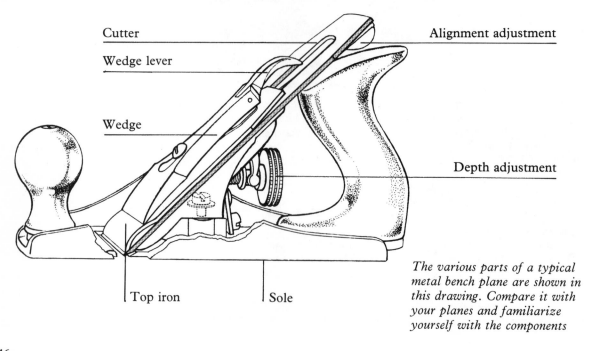

Cutter

Wedge lever

Wedge

Alignment adjustment

Depth adjustment

Top iron

Sole

The various parts of a typical metal bench plane are shown in this drawing. Compare it with your planes and familiarize yourself with the components

Chisels

You need chisels for certain shaping operations that other tools can't do, for cutting out recesses in wood for hinges, locks and similar fittings, and of course for cutting joints (Chapter 7).

There are two types of chisel, differentiated by the shape of their blades. The first is the firmer chisel, which has a blade of rectangular cross section. It is extremely strong, but has one drawback; it can't undercut. That's why the other type of chisel is the most versatile for everyday work. It is called a bevel edge chisel, because the outer third of the blade width has been ground back to a bevel at each side.

You may also come across mortise and paring chisels, and also chisels with curved blades, called gouges. The mortise chisel has a much thicker blade than the firmer and bevel edge chisels, and is used to cut mortises where considerable leverage sometimes has to be applied. The paring chisel is a bevel edge chisel with a long blade, and is used for cutting long grooves. Gouges are used to cut shallow indents and curved grooves, and to cut curves to match a mating rounded surface, where a rail meets a round chair leg, for example. They are the sort of tools you buy if and when you need them for special jobs.

Bevel edge and firmer chisels come in a range of widths, usually from $\frac{1}{4}$ in. (6mm) up to $1\frac{1}{2}$ in. (38mm). Very narrow chisels are rarely needed, and wider ones are expensive and awkward to handle. Start with two or three sizes, say $\frac{1}{4}$ in. (6mm), $\frac{1}{2}$ in. (12mm) and 1 in. (25mm), which will cope with most chiseling jobs.

Using a chisel

The first thing to do when you buy chisels is to sharpen them (page 48). The second thing is to remember two basic safety rules in using them. Always keep the cutting edge sharp. With a blunt tool you may force the cut, the chisel can slip and cut you or damage the workpiece. Always cut away from the body, with both hands behind the cutting edge. Then if you do slip there is no risk of cutting yourself.

The chisel's basic role is slicing away wood, either with or across the grain. Perhaps its simplest job is rounding off the corners of a piece of wood called "paring." To do this, place the workpiece on a piece of scrap board to protect the bench from chisel cuts, and place the chisel over the corner you want to remove. Grip the handle of the chisel with one hand, and use the other hand to guide the blade, using the weight of your shoulder to drive your top hand and the blade downward. Don't try to cut off too much at once; just keep shaving away at each fresh corner until you have cut back to the marked line.

Cutting out a shallow recess, for example to take a door hinge, is another common job for a chisel.

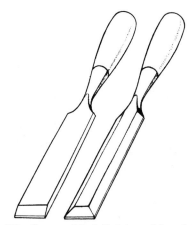

The firmer chisel (left) and bevel edge chisel (right)

After marking the extent and depth of the recess on the workpiece, cut around it, using the chisel vertically. Start the cut slightly inside the waste area, with the bevel pointing away from the cutting line, and use a gentler version of the paring technique to drive the chisel into the wood to the required depth. When you have cut all around the perimeter of the recess, start slicing away the wood in the center. Using the chisel horizontally, and with the bevel uppermost, let one hand provide the "push" while the other guides the blade. Begin to slice away the wood, a little at a time, letting the chisel cut slightly upward toward the back of the recess and being careful not to let it cut too far. Continue until you reach the depth line on the face of the work, then keep the chisel perfectly level to clean up the bottom of the recess.

47

Trim out any remaining wood fibers from the corners of the recess, and the job is done.

Taking care of your chisels
Keep chisels sharp, clean and free of rust, and protect them when they are not in use by fitting plastic blade guards. Most new chisels are supplied with them. Keep wooden handles sanded smooth and lightly oiled and plastic ones clean.

Right: paring is slicing away wood across the grain, here to round off a corner. The finger around the blade guides the cut.

To chisel out a recess, chop around the edges first and then use the chisel, bevel uppermost, to clean out the waste wood

Sharpening chisels and planes
To keep chisels and planes in tip-top condition you must sharpen them regularly, even during a job. To do this correctly you need an oilstone and some light machine oil, and an understanding of how the blades of chisels and planes are designed.

Both have two bevels on one side of the blade; a wide grinding bevel, at an angle of about 25° to the blade, and a narrow honing bevel at about 30° to the blade. The grinding bevel is already on the blade when you buy it, and will need regrinding only if the blade is damaged. You add the honing bevel as you sharpen the blade on the oilstone.

To get the angle right, and to prevent you from rounding off the end of the blade by rocking it unintentionally from side to side as you sharpen it, it's best to use a honing guide, a wheeled clamp that holds the blade at the correct angle and keeps it square to the stone. Get one that will hold plane irons as well as chisels.

Pour a little oil onto the stone, and put the blade in the honing guide, so that the grinding bevel is flat on the stone. Work the bevel over the whole area of the stone rather than just pushing it backward and forward over the same track. If you do you will wear a groove in the stone. Then adjust the blade in the guide so that you can form a new honing bevel, which will need just a few passes on the stone. Now run your finger down the flat back of the chisel. You will find that in sharpening the blade you have formed a tiny burr of metal around the cutting edge. Place the chisel flat side down on the stone, and rub gently to remove this; this will take only one or two strokes. Check that the burr is removed by running your finger over the beveled face of the blade. If it is not smooth, touch the stone lightly with the blade at the honing angle to get a new razor-sharp edge. Test it by cutting a hanging sheet of paper.

Store your oilstone in a box (page 149) and wipe it clean after use. If it should become clogged with oil, stand it in a metal tray in a warm oven to drain it. Then wipe it dry when it is cool.

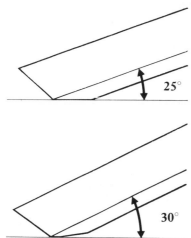

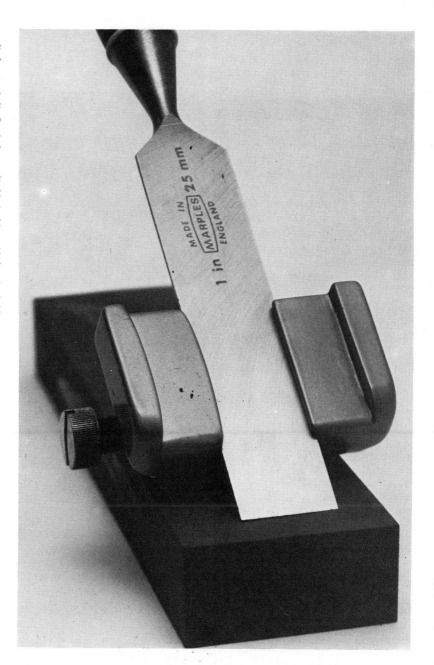

Above: the grinding angle (top) and honing angle (bottom) on a chisel blade. Right: a honing guide helps you to achieve the correct honing angle of 30°

Abrasive tools

This group of tools shapes wood by smoothing down its surface rather than by cutting it. The rasp and the file are the most common abrasive tools. There are also shaping tools called Surforms available for a wide range of shaping, especially on curves and internal cut-outs. These have teeth punched out of sheet metal, and they don't clog up since the fine shavings pass up through the holes in the blade. They remove wood extremely quickly, and when blunt or damaged can quickly be fitted with new blades. Both flat and round-bladed versions are available.

The rasp, now largely replaced by these shaping tools, has fairly coarse teeth. It leaves a rough finish which is then cleaned up with a file. Two file shapes are most useful, the half-round and the small-round, or rat tail.

Less common shaping tools

The spokeshave is a sort of plane for curves, and is used to trim curved surfaces after they have been sawn to shape with a frame saw. It must always be worked towards the end grain of the wood.

The cabinet scraper is a piece of tool steel, usually measuring about 2 × 4 in. (50 × 100mm), on one edge of which a slight burr is raised. It is used only on hardwoods, and is pushed across the surface of the wood at an acute angle to remove very fine shavings as the last stage in preparing the surface for finishing.

The half-round rasp is used to shape curved surfaces before they are smoothed to a fine finish with a file and glasspaper

The Surform comes in a wide range of shapes and sizes, and removes wood extremely quickly with its unique open cutting edges

Boring

Until the development of the power drill two tools were needed to bore holes in wood—the hand drill used for small holes, up to about $\frac{1}{4}$ in. (6mm) across, and the carpenter's brace for large holes, usually up to about 2 in. (50mm) in diameter. The power drill copes equally well with all but the largest holes, but there is a case for having a hand drill in your tool kit too.

The main reason is one of convenience. During a job, your power drill may already be in use with one of its attachments such as a saw or sander, and in this case you will save time by not having to dismantle it if you have another drill on hand. Also the hand drill can reach into tighter corners than a power drill, and can of course be used anywhere even if there is no electricity.

Hand drill

The hand drill is a comparatively simple tool. The crank is attached to a toothed wheel, which drives one or two pinions fitted to the body of the drill. The lower pinion drives the chuck around. The upper one is merely an idling pinion which helps to lessen wear on the mechanism and makes this type of drill, called a double pinion drill, stronger than a single pinion one. On some models the whole mechanism is enclosed in a circular casing, which has the obvious advantage that it keeps dust and wood chips out. It also means that it can be packed with grease.

The double pinion hand drill with a selection of the round-shanked twist drills it drives. The largest has a reduced shank

There are usually two handles, apart from the one on the crank. The top handle is for general use, and the detachable side handle for situations where restricted space makes the top handle difficult and awkward to use.

The hand drill is used with round-shanked twist drills, available in diameters from about $\frac{1}{16}$ in. (1.5mm) to $\frac{1}{4}$ in. (6mm). Fit these to the drill by undoing the chuck to open the spring-loaded jaws, then insert the twist drill and tighten up the jaws. You can drill either vertically or horizontally with equal ease, but the hole will be easier to start if you first make a small indentation with a center punch (page 57) at the point you want to drill.

Hold the drill at right angles to the wood, and start to turn the crank at a steady speed. Keep drilling until you have reached the depth you require (see depth stops page 54) or until the drill comes through the far side of the wood. On deep holes the drill may clog with wood chips. To prevent this, withdraw it from time to time by keeping the crank turning while lifting the hand drill away from the work. Simply pulling it out will leave the waste in the hole and may also break a thin twist drill.

The twist drills used with a hand drill may be made of carbon steel or what is called high-speed steel. The latter are preferable, if more expensive, for three reasons. They are stronger, last longer and can also be used with power drills. Carbon steel twist drills may snap at high revolutions. They can be sharpened when they become blunt using a special sharpening tool. Alternatively you can have drills sharpened by a professional.

A hand drill can also be used with a special bit that forms the cone-shaped recess (a countersink) necessary when using countersunk screws (page 90).

To use the hand drill, grip the top handle with one hand and turn the crank handle with the other. Don't press too hard; let the drill bit do the work, while you concentrate on keeping the drill vertical as you work

The carpenter's brace

To drill a large diameter hole in wood, you need more leverage than the hand drill can provide. The tool to use is the carpenter's brace. Work it by holding the top handle with one hand while you rotate the sweep handle with the other. The plain brace works with a continuous sweep; the ratchet brace allows you to turn the sweep handle through any angle, return it to its original position and then provide a further turn. It is ideal for work in confined spaces where a full sweep cannot be taken.

The chuck works in a similar way to that on the hand drill, but has two machined jaws designed to hold the square-shanked bits that the brace uses. There are several bit patterns. The most common is the center bit, which comes in sizes up to about 1½ in. (38mm) and is best used on thinner wood. It tends to wander on deep holes. The Jennings pattern is better for long holes, the Forstner bit is chosen when holes with flat bottoms are required, while the expansion bit does exactly what its name implies. It is adjustable and will bore holes up to a maximum of 3 in. (75mm) across. In addition, a countersink bit is available, and also a screwdriver bit which enables you to apply far more leverage than you can with an ordinary screwdriver. This can be as useful for removing stubborn screws as it is for driving them into the wood.

The main point to remember about using a brace and bit is that you will split the wood on the far side if you try to bore straight through it. Avoid this by drilling until the point of the bit penetrates the far side of the wood. Then reverse the workpiece and bore from the other side to complete the hole. This method will not work on thin wood, however. The answer here is to clamp the workpiece to some waste wood, and bore through the workpiece into the waste wood.

When using the brace and bit, check frequently that you are boring at right angles to the wood surface by sighting the bit against a try square or a scrap of wood held vertically in the vise beside the workpiece.

Using the brace and bit, with a piece of scrap wood held in the vise to serve as a vertical guide

A screwdriver bit used with the brace gives far more leverage than a hand-held screwdriver for driving stubborn screws

Depth stops

If you want to drill a hole to a certain depth instead of right through the wood, you need some way of knowing how far you have drilled. The simplest method is to wind a piece of adhesive tape around the drill. For more accurate work, the best answer is to drill a hole through a short length of square wood with the twist drill you'll be using to make the fixed-depth holes, and then cut the wood so that the twist drill protrudes from it to exactly the depth you want the hole to be. Don't worry if you cut it slightly the wrong size; altering the position of the twist drill in the hand drill's jaws will enable you to get the projection just right. Then when you drill, the block of wood rotates with the twist drill and when it reaches the surface of the workpiece you will have drilled a hole of exactly the required depth. Withdraw the twist drill as already described.

If you are using a brace and bit instead of a hand drill, the adhesive tape trick can be used on center bits and the Forstner pattern bit. However, it does not work very well with auger bits. In this case it is better to use a pre-drilled wooden block that is fitted over the bit in the same way as described for the hand drill. It must be cut accurately to length, though, as you cannot adjust the position of the bit in the jaws as much as you can with the hand drill.

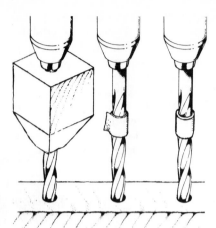

Three ways of improvising a depth stop for use with the hand drill; a block of wood (left), a piece of adhesive tape wound around the drill bit (center) or a piece of rubber or plastic tubing slipped over it (right)

Bradawl

Although not strictly a boring tool, the bradawl is included because its function is allied to the hand drill. It is a small pointed tool, rather like a thin screwdriver, used to make holes for starting screws. Use it by pressing it vertically into the wood where you want to drive the screw, and then turn it with a semi-rotary action. The sharp edge cuts into the wood fibers and the round shank makes a hole.

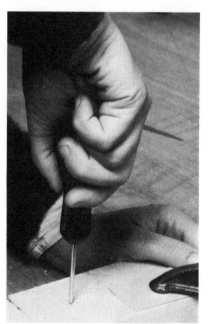

The bradawl is used to make starting holes for screws too small to warrant the drilling of pilot and clearance holes (page 89). It is used with a side to side twisting action

Joining tools

To join the pieces of wood which you have cut and shaped, you need one of three tools, according to the way you are to do the joining. The first is a hammer, for driving in nails.

There are several different hammer types, each with its own special usefulness. The best choice for the beginner is a claw hammer, which not only drives nails, but pulls them out too. To use it for driving nails, hold it near the end of the handle, thumb on top, and use it with a firm stroke, allowing your forearm to pivot from the elbow while keeping your eye on the nail head. This ensures that the hammer head meets the nail at right angles. This is not so easy if you pivot from the wrist.

The face of the hammer is slightly curved. As long as you hit the nail with the center of the face, you will be able to drive the nail almost flush with the surface of the workpiece without damaging it.

To pull nails out, hook the claw under the nail head and use a lever action to draw the nail out of the wood. You must be careful not to damage the workpiece. The best prevention is to slip a thin scrap of wood or sheet material under the hammer head.

Keep the hammer clean and free of rust. A dirty hammer always seems to bend nails. Oil wooden shafts lightly with linseed oil, and check from time to time that the head has not worked loose. If it has, drive the metal wedges securing it a little deeper into the end of the handle.

You will also find a small pin hammer invaluable. Driving small nails, pins and tacks with a big claw hammer is bad for your fingers and not very good for the nail either. Use the flat peen end of the hammer to start pins and then turn it around to tap the pin in. Or hold small pins in position by pushing them through a strip of sturdy cardboard so your fingers don't get in the way.

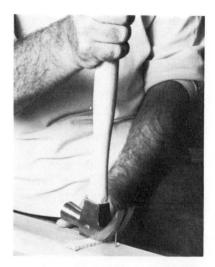

Right: protect the workpiece surface when extracting nails with a claw hammer.

Hold the hammer handle near its end and pivot from the elbow

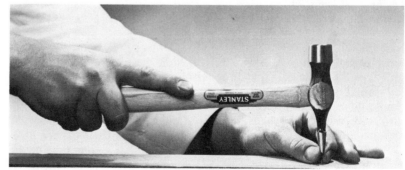

Start small pins using the flat peen end of the pin hammer

Screwdrivers

The second type of joining tool you need is a screwdriver; in fact, you may need several. Screws come in many different sizes and three distinct types. The most familiar is the slotted head. For successful driving, your screwdriver tip must fit the screw slot both in width and length. If it is too small you will damage the head of the screw, and if it is too large you will damage the workpiece as you make the last few turns. There are two types of cross-headed screw, the Phillips and Pozidriv patterns, each needing its own type of screwdriver. Whatever type you are using, the secret of successful screwdriving is to keep the tool vertical, using your other hand to guide the blade into the slot as you drive the screw.

Wooden mallet

Use the mallet mainly for tapping wood joints together (Chapter 7). Its other main purpose was once to drive chisels on deep cuts, because a hammer damaged the wooden handles, but now most chisels have plastic handles that can be struck with a hammer without splitting. You can use a hammer and a block of wood for joint assembly.

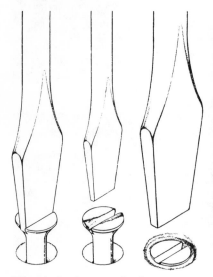

The blade tip must fit the screw head or damage will result

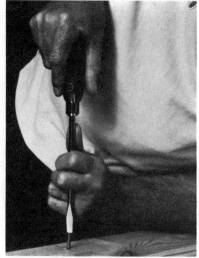

Hold the blade with one hand while the other turns the screw

Using a wooden mallet and chisel to chop out a mortise

Nail punch

A useful extra tool to consider for your tool kit is the nail punch or nail set. You can hammer nails almost flush to the surface of the workpiece, but to drive them down into the surface, use a nail punch. The best type has a concave end which fits over the nail head. Flat-ended punches can slip off the nail and damage the wood. If you want to hide the nail head completely, punch it below the surface by about $\frac{1}{8}$ in. (3mm) and fill the hole with wood filler (page 137).

Other joining-up tools you will come across are the ball peen hammer, which has a round peen, the Warrington hammer, a larger version of the pin hammer, and the ratchet and Yankee screwdrivers. The ratchet screwdriver works on the same principle as the ratchet brace, and can be used to drive screws out as well as in, by reversing the ratchet. The Yankee screwdriver combines the ratchet with a spiral push action and is far easier on the wrist if you have a great deal of screwdriving to do.

Miscellaneous tools

There are several other useful tools which don't fit into the categories I have covered. The center punch is another useful punch, used to mark the point where you are going to start drilling so that the drill point doesn't wander.

A pair of pincers is useful for pulling out nails that a claw hammer can't get a grip on. There is usually also a tack lifter in the end of one handle-grip, for lifting small tacks. Use pincers with a rolling action, gripping the nail head between the jaws and then rolling the jaws to one side to draw the nail out. Use a protective packing so you don't mark the workpiece.

The adjustable wrench is a clever combination of wrench and clamp which will do almost any job from tightening a nut when a wrench isn't handy to holding small sections of wood on your workbench. Add a pair of pliers, which you will need for routine jobs around the house.

A sanding block is also a useful item in the workshop. For hand sanding of wood surfaces, you will get a far better finish by wrapping the abrasive paper around a cork sanding block than you will by using the flat of your hand. In a pinch a scrap piece of wood will do instead.

Pincers are useful for pulling out pins and tacks a claw hammer cannot get a grip on. Pull small nails straight out; on larger or more stubborn ones; place a scrap of wood under the jaws and lever the nail out as if you were using a claw hammer

A last word on tools

When you are buying tools that you will use regularly, buy the best quality you can afford, which means buying a well-established brand. Other tools bought for particular jobs need not be of such high quality. You probably won't be using them very often.

Look after your tools when you have them. Don't knock bladed tools against each other, don't drop tools or throw them around and don't let them get rusty. Put them away as soon as you have finished with them.

Keep bladed tools sharp. They will perform better and you won't have to work so hard using them. Work with care whenever you are using cutting tools, saws and chisels in particular, by keeping hands away from or behind the cutting edge, and by keeping your eye on the job.

Don't let children play with your tools, unless you are prepared to take the time to teach them how each one should be used. Every child loves to help out in the workshop, and is likely to be fascinated by all the tools lying around. But the risk of an accident is always present. In fact, it's best not to encourage young children even to watch you at work. Even if they behave themselves, they will be a distraction that will certainly cause you to make mistakes, and may also contribute to a slip, a cut hand and a damaged workpiece.

CHAPTER 4
Power tools

There has been a revolution in home woodworking in the last twenty years, brought about by the availability of power tools. Of course, industry has been using machinery to take the effort out of working with wood for years before this, but the development of a small, portable electric power unit was the breakthrough that has changed home woodworking the most—for better or for worse, depending on whether you value the ease with which today's woodworker can carry out all sorts of complicated woodworking jobs more than the inevitable demise of the craftsman working with traditional hand tools. All in all, the balance comes down heavily in favor of power tools, which have enabled the home woodworker to carry out far more advanced and satisfying projects than were possible to anyone but the most dedicated craftsman with plenty of time on his hands. Power tools not only enable you to do things with an accuracy that only the most skilled woodworker could achieve with hand tools; they also enable you to do those things far more quickly.

The key to this power tool revolution is the electric motor, small enough to be built into a tool that can be held in the hand, yet powerful enough to be a viable alternative to hand tools. The first power tool to gain universal acceptance was a direct analogue of one of the most useful hand tools, the hand drill. The power drill first appeared as a single-speed electric tool for drilling holes in wood and has turned into a multi-purpose tool that not only drills through most materials thanks to a more powerful motor and a variable speed gearbox; it also acts as the power supply for a whole host of attachments that enable the woodworker to saw, sand, shape and polish his work with a minimum of effort. And by taking the development one stage further, the versatile electric motor now powers a whole range of separate tools that do the same jobs as the attachments, but do them better. You can even buy battery-powered tools too which run on rechargeable batteries so you can use them anywhere without having to trail cumbersome electrical cords after you. Power tools are a versatile addition to any workshop.

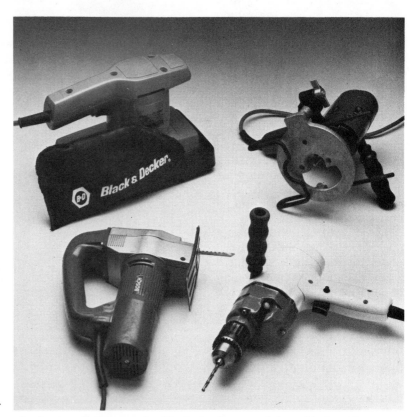

A selection of power tools. Clockwise from top left: orbital sander, router, drill and saber (jig) saw

The electric drill

Most electric drills look superficially very similar, but there are important differences between them. The type you choose depends on what you expect the tool to do for you.

The first factor is the drill's power, which is generally quoted in watts. The higher the wattage, the more powerful the drill and the longer it is likely to last you, since with extra power you are less likely to overwork the drill and risk burning out the motor.

The second point is the size of the drill's chuck, which refers to the maximum size drill shank that it will take. The smallest and least powerful drills have a $\frac{1}{4}$ in. (6mm) or $\frac{5}{16}$ in. (8mm) chuck, the largest a $\frac{1}{2}$ in. (12mm) chuck.

Third comes the drill's speed or speeds. Two-speed, four-speed and variable speed models are available. A single-speed drill will rotate at between 2500 and 3000 rpm, which is ideal for drilling, sawing and sanding wood, but with harder materials you risk burning out the drill bits. Better for all-purpose drilling work is the two-speed model, with a higher speed around 2400 rpm for working with wood, and a slower speed of about 900 rpm for drilling into masonry and also for drilling holes over $\frac{3}{8}$ in. (9mm) in wood. You select the speed you want by turning a knob or key. Variable speed drills have an electronic switch linked to the trigger, so that the more pressure you apply to it the faster the drill

goes, again up to a speed of 2400 to 2800 rpm. These drills are extremely useful for making an accurate start to drilling at low revolutions, and for drilling hard materials with smooth surfaces such as glass and ceramic tiles. Those drills with a built-in hammer action are intended for use in drilling into hard masonry.

For general purpose woodwork, and perhaps the occasional use with a sawing or sanding attachment, a 300 to 400 watt drill with a $\frac{3}{8}$ in. (9mm) chuck capacity will be adequate. Get a two-speed model so you can drill into masonry too; you are certain to have to do so at some time. For occasional drilling, a single-speed model with a smaller chuck will do, but don't expect too much power out of it. If you are going to be using power tools a lot you will probably be buying separate, integral power tools for sawing, sanding and so on. In this case you will use the drill only for drilling, and the two-speed model is the best tool to buy.

Battery-powered drills are less versatile as they don't have enough power to do much except fairly light drilling work. They can, however, power a variety of gardening accessories such as hedge trimmers and lawn shears.

Most drilling with a power drill is done with the same twist drills that fit the hand drill. But for larger diameter holes—up to 1 in. (25mm) across—you can buy flat wood bits. These have a center point to help in positioning the bit accurately

The versatile power drill

The first and most obvious application of the power drill is for drilling holes, mainly in wood. Electric drills use the same twist drill bits as hand drills, up to a diameter of $\frac{1}{4}$ in. (6mm), although you can get drills that will drill larger diameter holes and still fit the chuck. Because of the far higher speeds of electric drills, you will get longer life out of your twist drills if you buy bits made of high-speed steel instead of the cheaper carbon steel ones.

For larger holes in solid wood and the thicker sheet materials you can use auger bits, similar in pattern to those used with a brace, but with round shanks, or else flat wood bits, which will drill holes up to 1 in. (25mm) across. There are two kinds, the one-piece flat bit and the slotted shank with interchangeable drilling heads. With both of these bits, use a slow drilling speed for holes larger than $\frac{3}{8}$ in.(9mm). For drilling large holes in thin sheet materials, use an adjustable hole saw, a sort of toothed cylinder with a center guide bit, at the drill's slow speed.

If you are drilling holes you will probably need to countersink them for screw heads (page 90), and there is a special bit for that. You can also buy combined drill and countersinking bits, which do both jobs in one operation.

Using the drill

Since the power drill is really just a hand drill with a motor to turn the chuck, it's not surprising that you use it in much the same way for drilling holes in wood. To fit a twist drill, open the jaws of the chuck by turning the outer part counterclockwise. Insert the shank of the drill and then close the jaws by turning the chuck clockwise. Complete the tightening by using the chuck key in each hole in turn. Check that the bit is held square between the jaws.

It is easier to start the hole accurately if you use a center punch to mark the exact spot first. Hold the wood firmly in the vise. Then hold the drill next to your workpiece with the tip of the drill on the spot you have marked, and squeeze the trigger to start the drill, pressing firmly but not too heavily so that the drill begins to bite into the wood. Don't force it; let the drill bit do the work. If you are drilling right through the workpiece, approach the bottom of the hole slowly to avoid splitting the far side of the work, or else drill straight through it into waste wood beneath. On holes that don't go all the way through the wood, use the same type of depth stop used for hand drilling (page 54). When you have finished drilling, withdraw the bit with the motor still turning. This clears waste from the hole and stops the bit from sticking in the wood. This is particularly important when using thin drills, which may break if they are simply pulled out when the drill has stopped.

For more accurate drilling, you can use a drill stand. This device is screwed down to the bench and holds the drill exactly vertical. It is raised and lowered by means of a simple lever. You can preset the drilling depth, a valuable asset for repetitive work, and there is even a small vise which you can bolt to the base of the stand to hold small pieces of work securely while you drill them.

One criticism of the electric drill is that it can be awkward to handle in confined spaces, because it is bulkier than the hand drill. One way around this is to use a flexible drive shaft, a sort of wandering chuck that will reach into the most inaccessible corners. When you are using this attachment the drill itself should be held in a horizontal drill stand, a useful accessory which you can also use on the bench to leave both hands free when using attachments such as sanding disks and grinding wheels.

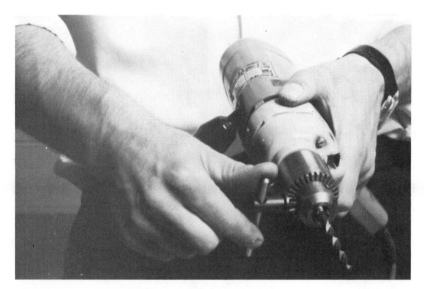

To fit a twist drill in the jaws, slip it into place to the correct depth and then tighten the jaws with the toothed chuck key

Use the detachable side handle to keep the drill vertical here

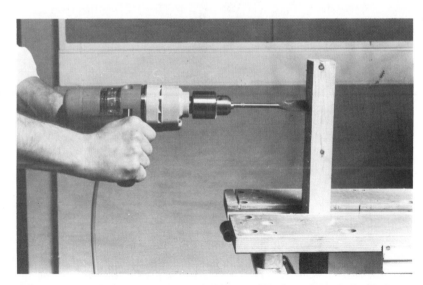

Clamp the workpiece securely in the vise or Workmate to drill a hole right through it. Again, the side handle steadies the drill

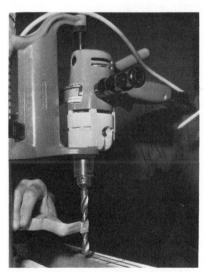

Use a drill stand and improvised depth stop for fixed depth holes

61

Specialized drilling

As well as drilling holes, the electric drill can power a range of rotary cutters. One is the plug cutter, which removes a neat plug of wood, like a short length of dowel, for use in hiding screw heads, for example. Another is the chisel attachment, a sort of rotating plug cutter that can be used for the sort of joint-cutting traditionally the province of the chisel. And most elaborate of all are the rotary milling heads with which you can cut grooves and make moldings of various sections.

Other attachments

You can also use the drill to power grinding wheels for tool sharpening, wire brushes for rust removal, polishing wheels for finishing work and even paint mixers. And you can buy an electric drill bit sharpener for keeping a good edge on your twist drills.

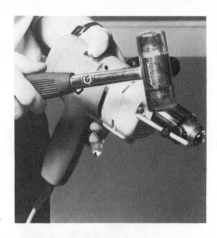

To remove the drill's chuck, insert the chuck key and tap it with a soft faced hammer

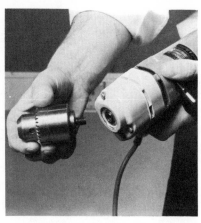

Once loosened, the chuck can be unscrewed by hand and replaced by the attachment you're using

A grinding wheel attachment is useful for sharpening the edge of screwdrivers, chisels and planes

This Easicut attachment works like a pair of electric scissors, and is used for cutting laminates

Milling attachments enable you to produce a wide range of edge profiles and moldings

Power sanders

Smoothing wood with abrasives before applying the finish is a time-consuming job. It is a perfect task for the labor-saving abilities of a powered sander. Because of the high speed of the sander, you can remove relatively large amounts of wood quickly with coarse abrasives, and also achieve a fast finish with the finer abrasives.

The simplest sort of sander is the disk sanding attachment, a rubber pad between 4 and 6 in. (100 to 150mm) across, with a metal back to which a shank is attached. This shank is usually a plain one like the end of a twist drill, and is fitted into the chuck of the drill in exactly the same way as a twist drill. The other type has a threaded shank, which you screw into the front of the drill in place of the chuck. The plain-shank type is more popular because it can be fitted so quickly, but it does not offer such a firm grip as the threaded type. The latter has the other advantage that the drill without its chuck is somewhat lighter to handle, an advantage on a long sanding job.

To fit the threaded-shank type of disk sander, you have to unscrew the drill chuck from its spindle. Insert the chuck key into one of the holes in the chuck, and give the shank of the key a sharp blow with a piece of scrap wood, in the direction in which the chuck rotates in use. You will then be able to unscrew the chuck by hand and remove it from the drill, and screw in the disk sander in its place. To

Circular sanding disks are held in place by a washer and screw

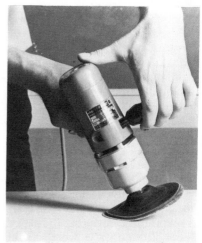

Hold a disk sander at an angle to the wood surface as you work

remove the disk when you have finished, give it a sharp tap on the perimeter so that you can unscrew it by hand and replace the chuck.

Fit the paper sanding disks to the rubber pad by unscrewing the machine screw and removing the dish-shaped washer underneath. Holding the disk in place, replace the washer and screw, making sure that they are fully tightened so that the screw head can't damage the workpiece in use.

Using a disk sander

The disk sander is used for smoothing flat surfaces. But it is not used pressed flat on the surface to be sanded. If it were, it would leave deep score marks which would be very difficult to remove. Instead, you must hold the pad at an angle of about 10 to 15 to the

surface, so that only one side of the disk touches it. Hold the drill with two hands. You will have better control if you fit the side handle. On a large piece of wood, start sanding at the edge farthest from you, and move the disk along slowly with the tilt in the direction of travel. Work in parallel strips, overlapping them just as if you were mowing the lawn, until you reach the other side of the board. On narrow edges, simply run the sander along the edge, holding it as before with the tilt in the direction of travel of the sander.

The disk sander is a fairly coarse tool, even when it is fitted with a fine grade of abrasive paper, and it must be used very lightly and carefully on work where a really smooth and score-free finish is required.

The drum sander

Obviously the disk sander can also be used to sand slightly curved surfaces, but on tight curves you can use an attachment called a drum sander instead. This is just a thick collar of foam plastic fitting around a smooth shank with a band of abrasive paper around the perimeter. With the shank inserted in the chuck of your drill, you simply run the edge of the drum around the surface you want to sand. Hold the drill firmly, so that the drum doesn't bounce around, damaging the workpiece or tearing the paper. When the paper is worn out or damaged, you can attach another band or else discard the complete drum and fit a new one.

You can use disk and drum sander attachments with the drill held on the bench in a horizontal drill stand. This leaves both hands free to manipulate the workpiece.

Orbital sanders

To get a really fine finish on wood you should use a finishing sander. This has a flat, rectangular rubber base pad which the mechanism rotates in tiny orbits, like hand sanding, but on a much smaller scale, so that the marks left on the surface are too small to be seen by the naked eye. The abrasive paper, about one third the size of a standard sized sheet of abrasive paper, is held over the base plate by clamps at each end.

Finishing sanders come as attachments for the electric drill, or as self-powered integral tools. The attachment is fitted to the drill spindle, so once again you will have to remove the drill chuck first. The one drawback with the finishing sander as an attachment is that running the motor for long periods, as you probably will for jobs like sanding down wall paneling or large sheets, means that the motor can overheat. Integral sanders are designed to cope with this, a good example of a specially designed tool being better than a compromise one. There are even finishing sanders fitted with a vacuum cleaner and dust bag.

Use a finishing sander in much the same way as you would iron a shirt, moving it up and down over the surface parallel with the direction of the grain while the oscillating base plate does the work. Don't press too hard as you work. You are not trying to remove as much wood as with the disk or drum sander, and you will find that the weight of the sander plus enough downward pressure to make it go where you want will be quite sufficient. On wide boards, hold the sander at a slight angle to the direction of travel, and overlap successive strips.

Drum sanders are perfect for smoothing curved edges

You can fit an orbital sander attachment to your power drill . . .

. . . or buy an integral powered orbital sander instead

Power circular saw

The circular saw takes the hard work out of sawing and produces cuts that are far more accurate than a hand saw. The simplest type of circular saw is an attachment designed to be powered by the electric drill.

This attachment consists of a casing into which the drill fits. The drill chuck has to be removed to allow the saw blade to be secured to the drill spindle by means of a hexagonal machine screw. There is a guide handle attached to the casing, and also a blade guard which fits over the lower part of the saw blade. This is usually spring-loaded so that it is pushed back when the saw is cutting, but springs forward again to cover the blade and protect the user as soon as the cut is finished.

Circular saw attachments usually have a 5 in. (125mm) diameter blade; however, don't be misled into thinking that you can cut very thick wood with it. In fact the depth of cut on such a blade is only about 1$\frac{3}{8}$ in. (35mm). The reason for this is the power available to drive the saw, which is that of the electric drill motor powering it. This may be as low as 250 watts, not enough to cut very thick wood. However, you could, if necessary, cut wood up to twice this thickness by sawing half way through it from one side, and then completing the cut by sawing through from the other side.

An alternative to the circular saw attachment is the self-powered integral tool. This has the same advantages over an attachment as integral sanders, because being designed to do just one job means that the motor can be more powerful and so the blade diameter and cutting depth can be increased. Integral saws are available with 7 in. (175mm) or even 8 in. (200mm) blades, which can cut thicker wood much more quickly than a 5 in. (125mm) blade powered by a smaller electric motor.

There are several types of blade for use with a circular saw. These are roughly equivalent in type to hand ripsaws and crosscut saws. The ripsaw blade has large, widely-spaced teeth, and is intended for cutting with the grain. The crosscut or fine-toothed blade has very small teeth, and is used for cutting across the grain of natural wood and for sawing up man-made boards. The combination blade cuts both with and across the grain, but does neither quite as well as the specialist blades.

Finally there are carbide-tipped blades, designed for use on chipboard, which with its high glue content quickly blunts untipped blades, and for cutting boards faced with plastic laminates.

Circular saw blades rotate in a counterclockwise direction when viewed from the "open" side. In other words, they cut on the upstroke, rather than on the down stroke as is the case with a hand saw. You can make sure that you have fitted the blade correctly by looking for the direction-of-

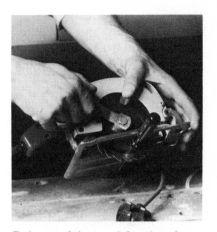

Before undoing or tightening the bolt holding the blade, push a screwdriver through one of the holes in the blade to stop it from rotating

rotation arrow that is printed on every blade; this should be on the open side of the saw. To fit the blade, put it in position and locate the hexagonal headed screw by hand. Then push a screwdriver through the hole in the saw blade and jam it against the sole plate of the saw to stop the blade from rotating while you tighten the screw. Make sure that the saw is not plugged in. To remove a blade, simply reverse the procedure.

How to use the saw

The basic cutting method with a circular saw is to pass the saw into the edge of the work, which must be firmly clamped down with enough clearance below it to allow the saw blade to protrude by about $\frac{1}{8}$ in. (3mm). Clamping the workpiece over two battens of waste wood is one way of doing this. Using a Workmate workbench (page 77) allows you to clamp the wood to one of the two long vise jaws, with the blade protruding into the space between the jaws as it cuts. Start the saw up away from the work, and then feed it into the cutting line steadily and firmly. Once the cut has started, apply a slight forward and downward pressure, the latter to cut vibration and to keep the sole of the saw flat on the work. As you near the end of the work, make sure the waste portion is well supported, and allow the saw to run clear of the wood so that the blade guard snaps into place before switching off the power. On long cuts, the sawcut can close up behind the blade and make sawing difficult. Stop the saw and insert a small wedge in the cut to hold it open before you continue. Making cuts in this way is not the most accurate method you can use. However carefully you use the line-of-sight guide on the saw to follow a pencil line on the wood, you are sure to wander a little, especially on long cuts. There are two ways of improving the accuracy of your cutting.

The first is to use a detachable

Set the blade depth so that it protrudes by about $\frac{1}{8}$ in. (3mm)

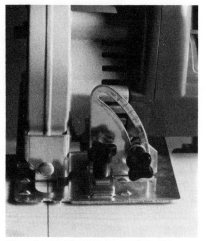

Use the guide mark on the sole plate to follow the cutting line

An adjustable fence makes accurate cutting much easier

Alternatively, run the sole plate against a long straight batten

guide called a fence. This is set to run along the edge of the workpiece, so that you can make a cut parallel with that edge and a preset distance away from it. It can be fitted to either side of the saw. The second method is to clamp a long, straight batten across the work-

piece and use this as a guide against which the sole plate of the saw can be pressed. This method is ideal for cuts on wide boards too far from the board edge for the fence to be used. In both cases, remember to take the width of the blade and the set of the teeth into

You can make angled cuts simply by tilting the sole plate

account when setting the distance between the intended cutting line and the guide batten or the edge of the work.

You will want to alter the depth of cut, according to the job you are doing. This is done by undoing a wing nut or a screw at the back of the saw and swinging the sole plate up or down according to whether you want a deep or a shallow cut. Check the cutting depth by resting the saw with its blade against the edge of the workpiece, adjusting the sole plate so that the lowest tooth just touches a line drawn on the edge of the wood representing the depth you want. Make sure that the nut or screw holding the sole plate is secure.

You can also make angled cuts with the circular saw, this time by undoing the blade tilt lock at the front of the saw. This allows the

saw to swing up to 45° from the vertical, and as with the depth cut adjustment must be firmly tightened before use. Once the angle is set, use the saw in the same way as for vertical cuts, with the fence, or using a batten as a guide. The sole plate remains flat on the workpiece. Of course, the blade cuts less deeply when it is set at an angle, a fact you must take into account when setting it up. The best way of checking the depth of cut then is to test it on a piece of scrap wood.

Saw benches
Instead of bench mounting the workpiece and holding the saw, you can reverse the procedure by using a saw bench. This is a metal table with a wide slot, underneath which the saw is clamped so that the tip of the blade protrudes through the slot. You adjust the depth of cut and the blade angle as before, but from underneath the saw table. The top of the table has an adjustable fence for straight cuts, and also a miter guide so you can make accurate cuts at angles other than 90°.

To make a straight cut, set the fence at the right distance from the blade. Then hold the wood against the fence, switch on the saw and push the wood steadily into the saw blade. For safety never do this with your hand. Use a push stick, a piece of scrap wood with a V-notch cut in one end. Use this method for cutting grooves too, setting the depth of cut accordingly and making several cuts to remove the

width of wood to make the groove.

To make cross cuts or angle cuts, use the miter fence as a guide, holding the wood at each side of the saw cut. Make your cutting mark on the leading edge of the wood, and then feed it into the blade, moving the miter guide along its slot as the cut proceeds.

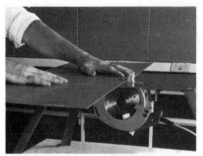

Feeding thin materials into the blade of a bench mounted saw

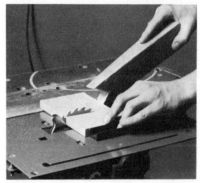

Always use a push stick to feed small pieces of wood to the blade

Power saber (jig) saws

The saber saw is like a small hand saw, since the toothed blade moves up and down in the same way as a hand saw does to cut the wood. Because the blade is relatively narrow, it can be used to cut straight lines or curves with equal ease, and can also make cuts in the center of the workpiece, something the circular saw *can* do with care, although only on long straight cuts. The saw cuts on the up stroke, which tends to pull the saw down into the wood. Then the down stroke pushes the saw up away from the workpiece, and the result is a tendency to vibrate which can only be prevented by a firm grip.

As with the circular saw, you can either fit a saw attachment to the power drill, or use an integral tool. With the former, the rotation of the drill spindle is translated into an up-and-down movement of the saw head. The cutting depth is usually limited to about 1 in. (25mm) in softwood, $\frac{3}{4}$ in. (18mm) in hardwood. The integral tool, with more power and designed for this purpose, can cut up to $2\frac{3}{4}$ in. (70mm) thick softwood and also thicker hardwood than the attachment, and is usually fitted with a tilting sole plate, like that on the circular saws, so that beveled cuts can be made with equal ease.

There is a wide range of blade types for use with the saber saw, ranging from a thin, fine-toothed $2\frac{1}{2}$ in. (63mm) blade for fine scroll-work up to a hefty 4 in. (100mm)

The power saber (jig) saw, a highly versatile integral power tool

blade for fast cutting of relatively thick wood. You can also buy special blades for cutting thin sheet materials such as plywood and plastic laminates, and hacksaw-type blades for cutting metal.

Using the saber saw

If you are starting a cut with the saber saw from the edge of the wood, rest the tip of the saw's sole plate on the edge of the wood, switch on and slowly push the blade into the cutting line. Then move the saw forward, maintaining a steady downward pressure to prevent vibration and letting the saw blade do all the work. If you

68

force it, the motor speed will drop, and you will risk damaging the motor.

Because the saw blade protrudes below the work, it is generally best to clamp it so that the waste side of the wood overhangs the edge of the bench. You will then have to support the scrap with your other hand as you complete the cut. It is easier if you work from right to left. Wedge open long cuts as you work to stop them from closing up and gripping the saw blade.

For long straight cuts, use the same trick to guide the cut as you did with the circular saw, clamping a long straight batten across the work, and running the sole plate of the jig saw against it. Set the distance of the batten from the cutting line with care, remembering to take into account the thickness of the saw blade.

For cutting curves from the edge of the work, the technique is exactly the same. However, since you will be cutting freehand, it is generally best to cut fractionally on the waste side of the guide line, so that any slight unevenness can be smoothed with a rasp or sander.

Being able to make cuts in the center of the workpiece is the other advantage of the saber saw. You can do this in one of two ways, either by drilling a pilot hole as you would when working with a coping saw, or by feeding the blade straight into the wood. Using a starting hole is probably safer for the beginner, especially on square holes where a drilled hole at each

corner of the cut-out means you can cut right up to them with ease. For plunge cutting, tilt the tool forward steeply, resting the forward edge of the sole plate on the work, and align the blade with the cutting line. Switch on and lower the blade into the wood, bringing the saw back to the vertical as the cut is started. Begin the cut an inch (25mm) or so from the end of the marked cutting line, and when you have reached the far end of the cut turn the saw around and return to the starting point to complete the other end of the cut.

For beveled cuts, simply set the sole plate to the angle you need using the scale on the saw, and lock it firmly in position.

Remember that because the saw cuts on the upstroke, you will get a slightly ragged edge on the upper surface of your workpiece. So if you are cutting wood or sheet materials with a "good" side, place the good side down on the bench with cutting lines marked out on the reverse.

Run the sole plate against a guide batten on straight cuts

Make plunge cuts by lowering the angled blade into the wood

On curves, cut just on the waste side of your marked line

Power routers

The router is a very useful power tool, a cross between the hand router plane and the electric drill, but much more versatile than either. The motor rotates at a far higher speed than any other power tool, around 30,000 rpm, and drives a range of special bits that can shape edges, cut grooves and rout out enclosed recesses that other tools cannot reach. It can also be used to cut a variety of woodworking joints.

The router consists of a motor unit and a base plate to which guide handles are usually fixed. The various cutting bits are slotted into the drive shaft and secured there by a nut so that they protrude through the base plate. A lock on the motor unit stops the motor shaft from turning when this nut is being tightened or slackened.

The router base slides onto the motor unit and is clamped to it by a knurled screw. Then the bits are inserted through the face plate and secured to the drive shaft by tightening the nut with a special wrench. It is obviously vital with the high speed of rotation the router uses that the bit is very securely fitted to the shaft. With the bit in place, the depth of cut can be set by sliding the base plate up or down until the bit protrudes from the face plate by the required amount. The clamp screw is then tightened to lock it in place. There is also some measure of fine adjustment on most models.

You can fit a guide fence to the router in the same way as for a circular saw, and use it to follow straight or curved edges, for example to cut a decorative groove around the surface of a table top. Straight cuts can also be made by running the router against a guide batten. You can cut smaller diameter circles without a guide edge by using what is called a trammel point, attached to one of the fence guide rods. This point acts as a center around which the router is swung in a circle. Its point holds it in the wood as you work. And you can even follow a metal or plywood template using a template guide, a thin metal sleeve through which the bit is inserted. This guide is kept firmly pressed against the template as the cut is made.

Router bits

There are many different-shaped bits you can use in the router, but they fall into two broad groups, groovers and edgers. Groovers cut square grooves, semi-circular grooves, V-shaped grooves and dovetail grooves, which are wider at the bottom than at the top. The edgers produce a straight edge, often as good as that achieved with a bench plane, a chamfered edge, a recessed edge and a wide variety of decorative moldings.

Most cutters are made in high speed steel, which is suitable for use on hardwoods and softwoods, but should not be used on plastic laminates or on chipboard, which will blunt the cutters quickly. For working these materials use tungsten carbide-tipped bits, which are more expensive than the steel ones but keep their edge much longer.

Using the router

The first thing to realize about the router is that because the cutting bit revolves clockwise as you look down on the tool, there is a tendency for the whole machine to drift to the left as you move it forward over the workpiece, or to the right as you draw it back. So if you fit a fence to work at a certain distance from the edge of your workpiece, you should always fit it to the right to prevent the leftward drift as you move the tool forwards. When you are using the router free-hand, keep up a slight angled pressure to counteract the drift, according to the direction in which you are working.

To start a cut, switch on the router and lower it into the work. Move it from left to right on straight cuts, counterclockwise on circular cuts and curves. Don't force the router through the work. It will pull itself through the wood once the cut is started, and all you need to do is guide it and provide the slightest downward pressure. If you push too hard you will overload the motor. If you push too slowly you risk burning the wood and overheating the bit so that it loses its tempered edges. At the end of the cut, switch off the motor and allow the bit to stop before lifting it from the work.

Always work in a good bright light so you can see precisely what you are doing, and turn the router slightly as you work if you find that the base plate obscures your view. Keep your bits sharp by touching up their cutting edges with a silicon carbide slipstone. Remove resin build-up by wiping the bit with a cloth moistened with a solvent.

As an alternative to holding the router in your hands, you can mount it upside-down in a router bench in the same way as a circular saw can be fitted into a saw bench. However, such benches have to be homemade, they are not generally available for use with portable routers. They work on the same principle as a saw bench, with the cutter sticking up through the bench surface and the work being fed through it, guided by a fence.

Using its special dovetailing attachment, the router makes light work of cutting perfectly matched dovetail joints

The power router will cut grooves in a variety of shapes and sizes

Specially shaped cutters enable you to produce elaborate edge profiles and moldings in a wide variety of patterns

71

Other power tools and accessories

There are a number of other power tools and attachments that you may want to add to your workshop. For example, you can buy an integral power plane; a grinder which is useful for sharpening edge tools such as planes and chisels, available as an integral tool or as an attachment for your drill; a lathe attachment for wood-turning work; a dovetailing attachment for making accurate dovetail joints; and even an attachment for snipping through plastic laminates. None of them do anything that you can't do equally well with hand or basic power tools, but they may be worth buying if you find yourself with large and regular amounts of work of a particular type where a power tool will mean you can work more quickly and effortlessly.

Above: the power plane makes light work of planing down even large pieces of wood like this

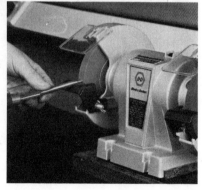

Right: regrinding chisel and plane blades is easy with a bench mounted power grinder

Safety with power tools

Power tools are designed to be as safe as possible, features like blade guards on circular saws and double insulation to lessen the risk of shock are intended to cut the risk of an accident to the user. But the manufacturer cannot legislate for careless and incorrect use of his tools, which is where the responsibility rests firmly on you.

For a start, look after your power tools. A correctly maintained tool will be safer than one that is dirty, damaged or falling apart. The plug should be an impact-resistant rubber one, the cord rubber-sheathed and unbroken. Don't pick up the tool by its cord, and keep the cord out of your way as you work. Coil it up neatly when you have finished using the tool; trailing cords are dangerous. Never use power tools in wet conditions.

When you are using any power tool, don't wear loose, floppy clothes or ties; they can easily get caught up in moving parts. Never try to brush away chips or sawdust from the vicinity of a saw blade, drill or other bit until you have switched the machine off and allowed the moving parts to stop. Then use a soft brush, an old paint brush, for example, rather than your fingers. Bit and blade edges can be sharper than you think.

Never remove safety guards from tools like circular saws and grinders, even if you think they get in the way. As you work, pay attention in case the tool jams in the work, and be prepared to switch off immediately if this happens. A broken drill or cutting bit, or piece of saw blade or grinding wheel can cause a nasty accident if it flies off at high speed. It's a good idea to wear simple goggles when you are using a grinding wheel, and to improvise a simple face mask when sanding in confined spaces where the dust can't disperse easily. The dust is very fine and can be choking.

With bench-mounted tools, make sure that the screws or bolts holding them are secure. Unplug any such tools as soon as you have finished using them, so that they cannot be switched on accidentally.

The biggest risk of all around your workshop is children. Never let them use power tools, unless they are working under your supervision and have been trained to use them correctly. Young children should not even have access to your workshop. They are fascinated by machines such as these, and you can't trust them not to touch something they shouldn't.

Maintaining power tools

Most big power tool manufacturers have a network of service centers where spare parts can be bought, and where the tool can be taken for overhaul or repairs when they become necessary. It's a good idea to have power tools serviced occasionally; the frequency obviously depends on how much you use the tool, but in the meantime there are a few simple things you can do yourself to keep your tools in good condition.

First, a couple of general points. Don't store your tools in a damp environment. Rust will do more damage than any reasonable amount of use will cause. Check the condition of the cord and its connections to the plug and the tool regularly. Frayed or damaged cord should be replaced, and loose connections remade. Always use cord clamps where they are provided to take any strain off the connection.

Electric drills

Drill motors collect large amounts of dust, which can eventually clog up air vents and get into working parts. Try holding the smallest vacuum cleaner nozzle you have over the air vents to suck out loose dust. Otherwise open the drill casing by undoing the retaining screws, noting where they go if they are of different lengths, and then pull away the motor assembly from the gear box. You may have to remove the carbon brushes from their housings first, and this is a

good opportunity to check them for wear and to replace them if necessary.

Now brush or wipe out the dust from within the casing and around the motor, using a stiff bristle brush or a rag as appropriate. Replace the motor and the carbon brushes, checking that they slide freely into their housings, and refit the casing before testing the drill. Lubricate the back bearing with a little light oil to ensure that it runs freely without overheating, but don't attempt to dismantle the gearbox unless you are familiar with such mechanical intricacies. It's packed with grease, and can be difficult to reassemble properly.

Keep the chuck free of rust by wiping it occasionally with light oil or petroleum jelly. And use only sharp twist drills with your power tools. Blunt ones won't drill cleanly, and in your efforts to make them do so you risk overloading and burning out the motor. This point applies too with any of the various attachments you may be using with the power drill.

Saws and sanders

Similar points apply to electric saws. Clean them out occasionally, lubricating bearings lightly and checking that all fixing screws are secure. Use only sharp blades, and make sure that their fixings are undamaged by wear or over-tightening.

Sanders need little maintenance, apart from an occasional cleaning and lubrication of the mechanism.

CHAPTER 5
Somewhere to work

If you are going to embark on woodworking on any reasonable scale, you have to find yourself somewhere to work. It's impossible to try to work on the corner of the kitchen table. You not only need a work area to call your own, where you can be sure of some freedom of movement and freedom from interruptions; you also need a storehouse for your tools and materials. You can't keep your tools in a closet and your wood under the bed forever if you plan to do woodworking.

The garage
Your garage, if you have one, is an ideal place for a workshop. It's solid, dry and spacious enough if the car isn't kept in it all day. It may even be big enough for you *and* the car to share it. Build a workbench across the back end as a permanent fixture, or if the length of your car won't permit this, construct a fold-down bench along one of the side walls. Some workbench ideas are described on pages 76 and 77. You can store your tools on racks or shelves on the garage walls, and keep your supplies of wood and sheet material slung up under the roof or stacked along the walls. If the garage doesn't have a window, consider knocking one into the wall above your workbench. If you have a prefabricated garage built of concrete slabs, contact the manufacturer to see if he can supply modular windows to replace some of the concrete panels.

The attic
If you don't have a garage, you could consider using the attic as a workshop. However, there are several disadvantages to this. The floor may have to be strengthened to carry the weight of you, your materials and your workbench. There is, in addition, the problem of access for large boards, which will have to be cut up first, and the twin problem of getting any bulky workpiece you've made back downstairs again. But if you will be woodworking on only a small scale, it's a possibility worth thinking about. If you do intend to use the attic, board over part of the floor after checking that the joists are strong enough, and line the roof slope with insulation. Put in a roof window if possible to give you natural light, unless there is already a window you can use. And provide a good ladder so you can get up and down safely.

The spare room
Another possibility for a workshop is to make use of a room within the house, maybe a spare bedroom, or better still a downstairs room not needed by the family. It will be a simple matter to install a bench and some storage facilities for materials and tools. Everything else from windows to power supplies will already be there.

The basement or the shed
If you have a basement, this can be converted to a workshop in the same way as a room elsewhere in the house. The main drawbacks are that it may have little or no natural light and ventilation may be poor. Access may not be easy either, as winding stairs are not easy to negotiate with large boards and big workpieces.

An alternative is to use an outbuilding or shed as your workshop. Brick or concrete buildings will be warmer and more secure than wooden ones. You will have to take power and lighting out to the shed from the house and provide some form of safe heating if you want to use it in the winter.

The nomad
If there's literally nowhere you can set up camp around the house or in the yard, all you can do is equip yourself with a portable workbench and an extension cord for your power tools, and use closet space somewhere around the house to keep your tools. You'll have to buy materials as you need them.

The attic is ideal for small-scale woodworking activities

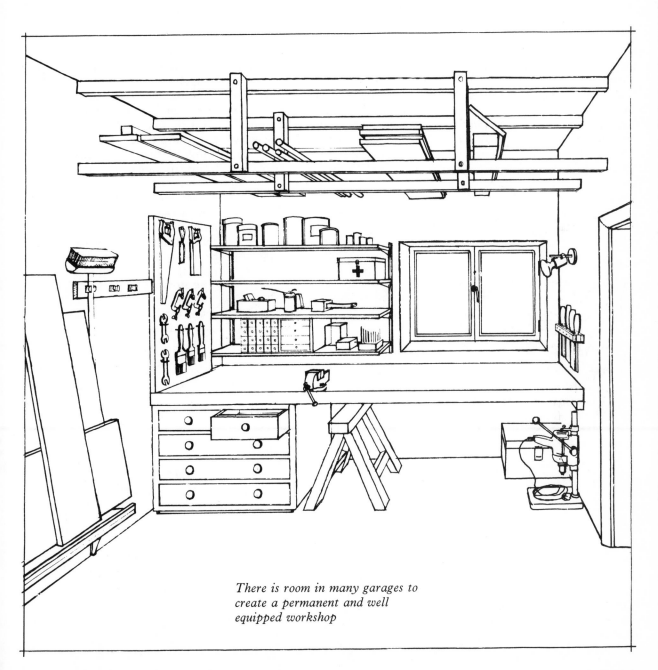

There is room in many garages to create a permanent and well equipped workshop

The workbench

A bench to work on is an essential part of any woodworker's equipment. From first measurement and roughest sawing to the most intricate joint cutting and careful finishing it acts as a support for workpiece and tools alike. The traditional woodworker's bench is a wood structure with sturdy legs, rigid enough to take heavy work without moving or vibrating unduly. It's usually free-standing.

The most important dimension of the workbench is its height. If this isn't right, you will find working for any length of time very uncomfortable. As a rough guide, the bench height should be the length of a chisel below your elbow when you are standing upright. This allows you to work as comfortably on the bench top as at the vise. Length is also important, but must be a compromise to suit the space available. Try to have a minimum of 4 ft. (1220mm) to give adequate support to large workpieces, and make sure there is reasonable clearance beyond each end of the bench to allow you to maneuver long pieces of wood or sheet material. The width should be about 2 ft. (610mm), again so that there is enough width to

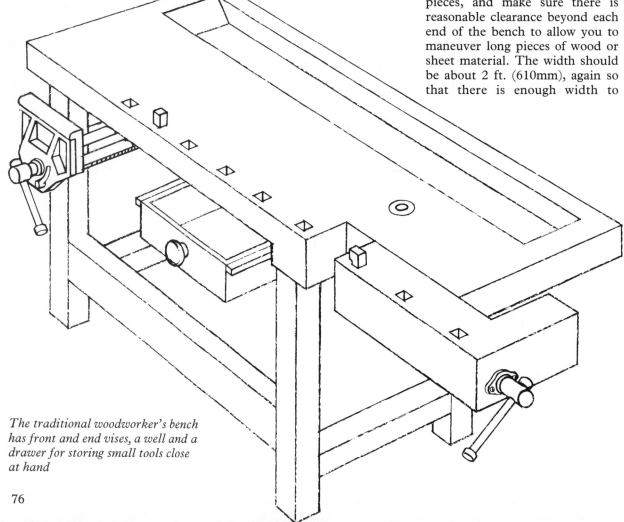

The traditional woodworker's bench has front and end vises, a well and a drawer for storing small tools close at hand

accommodate the workpiece. The front section of the bench is the prime work zone. The recessed area behind, called the well, provides a safe resting place for tools while you are working, stopping them from rolling off the bench.

The top of the bench should be at least 1½ in. (38mm) thick so that it gives good support to the work. It's usually made of beech, which stands up to heavy use yet is resilient enough not to bruise work or damage tools placed on it. It should have an overhang at the front and the ends to allow you to clamp work to it. Many firms make traditional wooden workbenches of this type, some simple and some quite elaborate, with built-in vises, storage space, tool racks and other bench aids. If you can't afford one, it's quite easy to build an acceptable substitute yourself. The basic requirements are sturdy legs, a strong solid top and enough cross-bracing to keep the structure rigid in use. There is a design for a workbench on page 154 that meets these requirements perfectly and can be made quickly and easily.

Instead of buying or building a free-standing bench, you may prefer to have a wall-mounted one that can be folded up out of the way when you have finished working. This, too, is quite easy to make. The three main requirements are a strong, rigid top, a sturdy front frame and a secure support for the hinged rear edge of the bench. The top can be made easily from two sheets of blockboard, and should

be stiffened along its front by the addition of a length of 2 × 3 in. (50 × 75mm) screwed to the underside about 4 in. (100mm) back from the front edge. The legs should be of 3 in. (75mm) square wood, linked by two cross-braces of 1 × 3 in. (25 × 75mm) wood notched into the legs. This frame is then hinged to the underside of the stiffening batten below the work-top. At the back of the bench a sturdy wall batten is fixed to the wall with screws and wall plugs, and the rear edge of the top is hinged to it so that when the top is lowered for work, its rear edge still rests on the batten. A couple of strong hooks and eyes hold the bench up against the wall when it's not in use, and bolts at the base of the two legs locate in holes in the floor or in wood blocks fixed to it, to make the whole structure rigid and safe to use.

If you prefer a portable workbench instead of a fixed one, there is a tailor-made answer in the Workmate. It's a metal-frame construction with a worktop that is in effect two long vise jaws that can either support flat work or hold it firmly. The whole bench can be folded flat for carrying or storage.

Although not really a workbench, there is another piece of equipment that's very useful if you will be sawing up long lengths of wood or board—the sawhorse. A pair will support large workpieces while you saw. You can easily make yourself a pair, either from sawn wood or from slot-together board components (page 152).

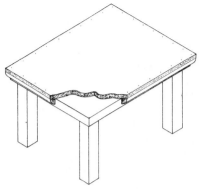

Improvise a workbench by covering a kitchen table with a board

The Workmate is the perfect portable workbench. It is available in several different models

77

Bench aids

Apart from the workbench, the woodworking vise is the most important piece of equipment in the workshop. Without one you will never be able to carry out more than the roughest and most rudimentary work, because almost every woodworking operation requires you to hold the workpiece firmly while you work on it.

There are two things to remember about vises. The first is that to grip large workpieces, the vise must have fairly wide jaws. It's no good trying to hold a door while you plane its edge in a vise that grips only a few inches of one edge. The second is that the vise is for gripping wood, not crushing it. The screw doesn't need to be tightened up as hard as it will go to hold the work securely. If you do this, you will certainly mark the workpiece, and possibly damage the vise mechanism.

There are several types of woodworking vise. The oldest is the wooden vise, built into the workbench and in effect an extension of the work surface. It is usually found fitted at the right-hand end of the bench, where in conjunction with aids called bench stops it is used to secure boards of various lengths on the bench top.

Another common type is the bench vise, which is mounted below the front edge of the bench with its jaws level with the bench top. The screw mechanism is underneath the bench, with only the outer jaw and the handle protruding. The inner jaw is usually let into the face edge of the bench so that work can be held right against the edge of the bench, effectively making one jaw of the vise as wide as the bench is long, and so providing a very firm grip on long boards. Although they are made of metal, the jaws are protected with wood facing blocks to minimize the risk of marking the work. A vise of this sort can hold wide pieces of wood with ease, and may be fitted with a front stop so that it can be used to clamp wood too wide for the jaws against another bench stop placed near the back of the bench. In addition, it will probably have a quick release lever so that you can run the outer jaw in or out without having to turn the handle round and round. This is done just for the last few turns needed to secure the workpiece.

A smaller version of this is the amateur woodworker's vise, which also bolts to the underside of the bench. It should also be fitted with wooden jaw facings, and should have the inner jaw let into the edge of the bench. It will not be able to handle wide pieces of wood.

If you don't have a permanent workbench, you could instead use a portable clamp-on vise. This fits over the edge of the surface you are using as a bench, where it is secured by a clamp tightened from below. If you are using it on a table or similar support, fix the vise as nearly over a leg of the table as you can for maximum support.

If you have a Workmate you won't need a vise. The jaws open to about 4 in. (100mm), but by using pegs in the holes cut in the vise faces, work up to 10 in. (250mm) wide can be accommodated.

Above: the portable vise can be clamped anywhere. Below: the bench vise is a permanent installation

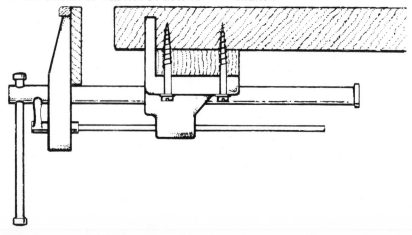

Bench stops and holdfasts

Bench stops are nothing more than raised pegs of wood or metal set in the bench top against which the workpiece can be pushed as you work on it. Wooden stops are pegs of hardwood about 1 in. (25mm) square, fitting through matching holes in the top of the workbench, and held in place by a wing nut underneath the bench so that they can be raised above the bench surface when they are needed and dropped flush with it when they are not. Metal stops are toothed wedges let into the bench top. They can be lifted up for use and laid flat afterwards.

A single bench stop can be used to plane against. Rest the wood against the stop, and use the plane so that it pushes the wood against the stop with each stroke. Pairs of stops, one on the bench and the other on the movable jaw of an end or front vise, are used to hold the workpiece at both ends, much more firmly than using a single stop.

The holdfast is an adjustable, L-shaped metal bar, useful for holding workpieces which are too small to be gripped between bench stops. The long stem of the L fits into a metal-lined hole in the bench top, and the short arm, with a swivel-mounted pad at its end, holds the workpiece against the bench surface. Because the stem hole is angled, tightening the screw on top of the holdfast pulls it tightly down on to the workpiece while the stem grips the sides of its hole securely.

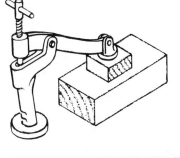

Above: the holdfast is a useful way of holding small workpieces on the bench top. Right: bench stops hold long workpieces securely along the bench front

Bench hooks and shooting boards

The bench hook is an invaluable aid for sawing small sections of wood on the bench top, usually with the tenon saw. It is not intended as a saw guide but more as a way of holding the wood securely while you work and of protecting the bench surface. It consists of a flat base to which two blocks are fastened to make the shape shown. You can buy a bench hook or make your own (page 146).

Use the bench hook with its base resting on the bench top and its lower block overhanging and butting up against the front edge of the bench. It can also be held in the jaws of a bench-mounted vise. The wood to be sawn is held against the rear, upper block and the pressure that you exert in that direction holds the wood securely while you saw. Note that the right-hand end of each block is cut away slightly so that the saw cuts down into the disposable bench hook instead of the indispensable bench top. By cutting away the end of both blocks, the hook can be reversed and its useful life doubled. If you are left-handed, cut away the left-hand end of the blocks instead of the right-hand end.

The shooting board is another wooden bench aid designed to help in the planing of end grain, which is a slightly tricky operation that can split the wood if you are not careful. The drawing overleaf shows how it is used and on page 151 you will find instructions on how to make your own shooting board.

The miter shooting board is an extension of this idea, designed this time for accurate planing of mitered angles, again without the risk of splitting the end grain. It is reversible, enabling you to plane miters in either direction. This is essential when working on elaborate moldings that cannot be reversed in position.

Miter blocks and miter boxes
Both of these tools are used to assist in the accurate cutting of mitered corners with the tenon saw. The miter block is very similar in principle to the bench hook, but has a thicker upper block in which two accurate 45° guides have been cut. The piece to be mitered is held against this block with a cutting mark in line with one of the saw guides, and the saw is then placed in one of the guides to keep it at the correct angle while the cut is made. The miter block is accurate only for wood of small cross-section, light beadings and picture frame moldings, for example. For larger pieces, the miter box is used. This has saw guides on both sides of the cut, and so is more accurate than the miter block. It can be used on wood sections up to the internal width of the box, with the saw running in opposite pairs of guides. These do not always extend to the bottom of the box. You should always remember to place a piece of scrap wood in the bottom of the miter box to prevent the saw from cutting into its base as the cut is completed.

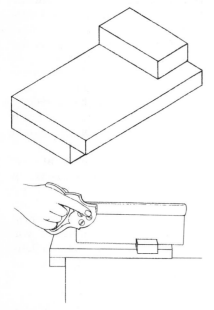

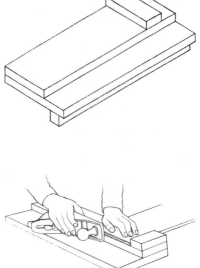

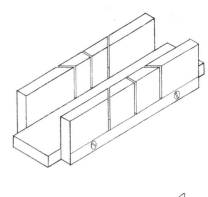

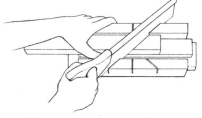

The bench hook is one of the simplest and most useful bench aids. It is held against the edge of the bench, and the wood to be sawn is held against the upper stop with the free hand

The shooting board is used mainly for trimming the ends of wood square, and also for planing the edges of thin pieces of wood that cannot readily be held in the vise or by bench stops

The miter box is used for cutting miters in small sections of wood and in moldings, particularly for picture frames. The two center guides allow you to make right-angle cuts too

Clamps

Clamps of various sorts are extremely useful both for holding workpieces on the bench for cutting and shaping, and also for holding various components together during final assembly. There are several types of clamp that are useful for the home woodworker.

One of the most popular for small-scale work is the C-clamp, which is used for holding small glued parts together and for bench clamping. Sizes range from about 2 in. (50mm) up to 12 in. (305mm), both measurements refer to the thickness of wood the clamp can hold. Some types have a swivel plate on the end of the screw, which is useful for holding tapered or other irregular sections.

Similar in purpose is the quick-action clamp, which has now largely replaced the old-fashioned hand screw for bench work. Its lower jaw can slide freely along the stem of the clamp, but is locked against it when the screw is tightened on the workpiece in much the same way as the holdfast is locked into its bench hole. All you do is slide the jaw up until it meets the work, and then give the screw a couple of turns to tighten it up.

A variation on the C-clamp is the edge clamp, which has a second screw at right angles to the main one. It's invaluable for holding edges of veneer or laminate in place while the adhesive sets.

The corner clamp or miter clamp is a simple device for holding the two parts of a miter joint firmly together for gluing and pinning. One screw holds the two components against the inside corner of the clamp.

For large scale work, joining boards edge to edge to make a table top, for example, or on box or frame constructions, you need some long clamps or sash clamps. These are so-called because they were widely used by carpenters to hold window sashes squarely and securely after assembly. The clamp consists of a flat or T-section bar fitted with two jaws. One is locked into place on the bar by a steel peg fitted through one of the evenly-spaced holes along the bar. The other is fixed at one end of the bar, but can be moved in and out by means of a screw. The movable jaw is positioned so that the work fits in the clamp with the adjustable screw fully out. The screw is then tightened to clamp the work securely between the two jaws. These clamps are usually used in pairs or threes, according to the size of the work to be clamped. Those with T-section bars are stronger than those with flat bars, and should be used for the heaviest work. One point to remember when using either type is that the strength and weight of the clamps can pull or force the work out of true, so don't over-tighten them, and check the work shortly after you have clamped it up to make sure this hasn't happened.

Whatever type of clamp you are using, always use small packing pieces of cardboard or scrap wood between the clamp jaws and the workpiece to protect the surface from marks.

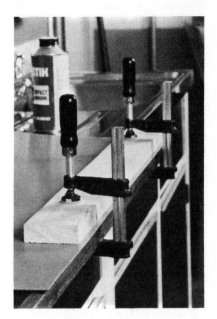

These quick action clamps are perfect for clamping plastic laminate in place on a worktop, and also for holding workpieces on the bench. The movable jaw slides freely along the stem, but is locked against it when the turnscrew is tightened on the surface of the workpiece

Storing tools

As your collection of tools and woodworking equipment grows, it is essential to organize some sort of permanent storage for them. If you don't they will get damaged and they will also probably get lost.

Because of the widely differing shapes and sizes of woodworking tools, storage must be flexible. The first thing you have to decide is whether you are going to make your own storage or rely on buying ready-made cabinets. Making your own allows you to create storage to meet your specific needs. Here are some storage projects that you can easily make yourself, using mainly wood scrap pieces.

Bladed and pointed tools such as chisels, screwdrivers, squares and files are best stored in a wall-mounted wooden rack, made from two softwood battens held about $\frac{1}{2}$ in. (12mm) apart by wood spacer blocks and subdivided into sections by dowels. The rack can then be bored through the spacers and screwed to the workshop wall, preferably just above the rear edge of the workbench. Unless your chisels have individual plastic blade guards, it's a good idea to fit a cover panel to the front of the rack for additional protection. If you use a piece of clear plastic you will still be able to identify each tool at a glance. You can also store small tools like bradawls and punches in a rack of this sort if you drill holes of the appropriate size in a strip of plywood and pin this to the top of the rack.

It is important to store saws correctly as damage to the saw teeth must be avoided. The best way of doing this is to hang saws on the workshop wall. Drill angled holes in a panel of $\frac{3}{4}$ in. (18mm) thick chipboard and insert 2 in. (50mm) lengths of $\frac{1}{4}$ in. (6mm) dowel into the holes so that they stick out at a slight upward tilt. Then screw the panel to the workshop wall and hang your panel and tenon saws on the pegs by their handles, two pegs to a saw. Coping saws should be suspended by their frames.

There are a number of other

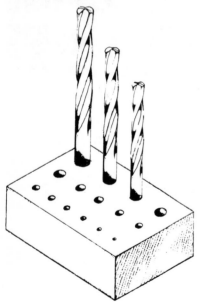

Make a small wooden block to store your twist drills neatly

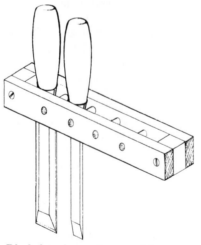

Bladed tools can be stored in simple racks made up from softwood pieces and short dowels

Wire hooks fitted into a pegboard make an inexpensive rack

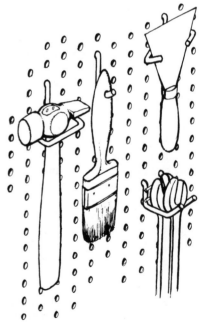

awkwardly-shaped tools which you can store in this way, like large squares, hand drills, braces, hammers and clamps. To ensure that each tool is put back in its correct place, draw silhouettes around each one on the board or label each set of pegs.

Planes should not be hung up. There is too great a risk that they will fall or be knocked down. And they don't have a convenient hanging handle. It's best to keep them in their original boxes, on their sides, not on their soles, and to keep the boxes on a shelf or in a drawer.

Small tools, metal rules, marking gauges and knives, for example, are best stored in a small handy drawer under or near the bench. This can also be used for storing spare parts such as coping saw and knife blades, and accessories like honing guides. If your twist drills and other bits are in a box or a plastic container, keep these there too. Otherwise make up storage blocks for them by using each drill bit in turn to bore a hole in a piece of hardwood, and then slot each bit into its appropriate hole.

Power tools are awkward to store neatly. Either keep them in a closet, or put up a wide shelf with a beading lip along the front edge, and line them up out of reach of children, with their cords neatly coiled around the body of the tool to avoid tangles. Remove blades and bits before storing.

If you prefer to buy storage equipment, there is a wide range of metal or plastic racks, clip boards, peg board and cabinets on the market. Buy equipment which is sturdy enough to take the weight of your tools and which will give you enough space for your tool collection to grow.

Small tool kits
If you are a small-scale woodworker and you have no permanent workshop, either adapt some of the earlier ideas to set up storage in a closet, or else invest in a tool box or tool bag. Both suffer from the drawback that tools can get knocked together, but some simple cloth packing will lessen the damage. Smaller tools can be kept in cloth rolls, especially suitable for chisels, screwdrivers and drill bits.

Storing miscellaneous items
Apart from your tools and wood, you will also need to keep quantities of hardware and other odds and ends in your workshop, and bundling them all together in a drawer or a box isn't the answer. You need individual storage compartments for several types of nails and screws, adhesives, fittings and so on. These can be improvised by a row of clearly labeled cans on shelves, or you can fit a row of glass jars to a shelf with their tops fixed to the underside with two screws.

If you prefer to buy storage cabinets, look out for compartmentalized boxes, or the small plastic drawers that interlock to build up a stack as big as you need. Label them clearly.

Power and light in the workshop
Unless you steadfastly refuse to use power tools, you will need at least two outlets in your workshop, preferably on the wall just above the workbench. Make sure that they are correctly installed as extensions of the house wiring by having an electrician install them for you.

Lighting is just as important as power. You can't rely on natural light being good enough to work by, and you are sure to want to use your workshop after dark. You need bright light falling onto the bench at the same angle as daylight, which means installing the light fixtures over the window. Use light bulbs rather than fluorescent tubes, as fluorescent tubes cast no shadows and make accurate work difficult. They also make wood colors look false. If the light fixtures can be adjustable, so much the better.

Total safety
There are three other things that no workshop should be without. The first is a first aid kit, which should be on display and easily reached. You never know when accidents will happen, however careful you are. Next is a fire extinguisher. Sawdust and fine wood shavings can be extremely flammable. Finally, always keep a flashlight handy, just in case you are plunged into darkness by a power cut, or need to find a screw behind the workbench.

CHAPTER 6
Fixing and fastening

The problem of joining wood to wood and to other materials has exercised the mind of the woodworker since the earliest days of the craft. Wooden artefacts found in Egyptian tombs show that some solutions to the problem had already been found, yet even today we are discovering new ways of making strong and long-lasting fixings with wood.

There are two main ways of tackling the job. The first is to use a device to make the bond. Examples include adhesives, nails, screws, dowels and a number of specialized fixtures. The second is to cut the wood itself so that the interlocking surfaces form a firm, strong bond or, in other words, wood joint. The two methods are closely linked, since while the various devices can make a bond without the help of a specially-cut joint, and some joints will hold without a device to strengthen them, the two are usually used together. This chapter will discuss adhesives, nails and some of the other pieces of hardware used in woodworking. The various types of woodworking joint are covered in Chapter 7.

Adhesives
Gluing wood together with an adhesive is perhaps the oldest form of wood-to-wood bond. The Egyptians knew how to make two kinds of glue which have hardly changed over the centuries; animal glues, made by boiling up hide and bones, and casein glues, derived from milk. Until the industrial chemist developed the synthetic adhesives about 40 years ago, these glues were still the standard ones used by the home woodworker, and they are still used today, particularly in the restoration of old work originally made with them.

For a glued joint to be effective, several criteria have to be met. The kind of wood can be important. Generally softwood is easier to glue than hardwood, and sapwood is easier to glue than heartwood because in each of these the glue can soak into the coarser grain of the wood. Oily woods like teak are notoriously hard to glue well. Moisture content is important too. It is virtually impossible to glue damp wood, and for best results the moisture content should be between 10 and 12 per cent, about the level found in woodwork and furniture in a well-heated house. The surfaces to be joined must be a close fit. Few adhesives will fill gaps and still produce a good bond. The strength of the adhesive must be matched to the strength of the wood, a point well illustrated by joining two pieces of balsa wood with a modern woodworking adhesive and then pulling them apart again. It's the wood that fails, not the adhesive, because the latter is stronger.

Even the way the adhesive is applied, held during setting and treated afterwards can affect the strength and durability of the bond. There is much more to using adhesives correctly than you might think at first glance.

Woodworking adhesives fall into six main groups: animal, casein, contact, epoxy, polyvinyl acetate and resin adhesives. Each has its own special advantages and uses. But first, here are some general points to remember about adhesives, whatever type you are using.

Surfaces to be joined should be clean, dry and free of grease. Except when using the contact adhesives, joints should always be clamped until the adhesive has set. And above all, the manufacturer's instructions for a particular adhesive should always be followed to the letter. Note especially any advice on how long the glue will keep if it is unopened and how long it lasts once opened or mixed. Make sure you know how to get it off your hands and other surfaces.

Animal glues
Animal glue, commonly called Scotch glue, comes in the form of granules or sticky sheets. You have to break it up first, soften it and then dissolve it in hot water to make it usable. Cover the glue with water in a jar or can, and then warm this in a pot of hot water, stirring all the time to dissolve the glue. When the glue runs off the spoon like syrup, it is ready for use. But it must be kept hot in order to be usable. That's why old-fashioned woodworkers always had a glue pot warming in the corner of the bench. What is more, you should really warm the wood too, so that

the glue doesn't cool too quickly. The bond will break easily if it does. Apply the glue to the joint with a brush, wiping away any excess glue quickly with a damp rag so it doesn't stain the wood. Then clamp the wood firmly until the glue has set. The bond, once set, is very strong, but it is not water or even damp resistant.

Animal glue does have one big advantage. It can be easily unmade again, by simply heating the joint until the glue softens. This makes the dismantling and repair of old furniture and veneer work much easier. If you are using Scotch glue for repair work of this kind, remember that you must remove all the old glue before brushing on a fresh coat, or it won't stick.

Casein glues

Casein glues are sold as fine powders which you mix with water and use cold. Unlike animal glues, the adhesive has no natural stickiness, and so rubbing joints together to get a good bond is no use; the joints must be clamped firmly. The joints are damp resistant, but not water resistant, although the bond strength recovers after the damp dries out of a dampened joint.

The adhesive dries pale yellow and can stain some woods, so it is important to wipe away any excess before it sets. The setting time is quite short. It will keep as a powder for up to a year, but once mixed must be used quickly. It is advisable to wear gloves when using it, as it tends to irritate the skin.

Casein glues are used for general interior work, and for sticking wood to cloth, leather, cork and linoleum. Other modern adhesives are, however, taking their place for these jobs.

Contact adhesives

These ready-mixed adhesives work in quite a different way from other adhesives. You coat the two surfaces to be joined with a thin film of adhesive, and then leave them separated until the solvent has evaporated and each surface appears to be dry. Then you press the two surfaces together and the adhesive films bond immediately. Because of this, the chief use for contact adhesives is in sticking plastic laminates and similar sheet materials to wood. They aren't very good for making woodworking joints, especially if the joint is under stress, as the adhesive can stretch and allow the joint to move.

Accurate positioning of the parts being joined is crucial because of the instant bond, and for this reason the slip sheet method of fixing is usually used. This involves placing a sheet of waxed paper between the two surfaces, and then gradually withdrawing it as the two surfaces are pressed firmly together. Once the bond is made, clamping is not necessary.

One word of warning is necessary about these adhesives. The solvent is acrid to inhale and is also flammable, so it should be used in an area with plenty of ventilation and no open flames. Some recently available adhesives are water-based and do not suffer from these drawbacks.

Epoxy adhesives

These are one of today's miracle adhesives, since they will stick almost anything to almost anything else. Also the bond is heat-proof and waterproof, as well as being immensely strong.

These adhesives are two-part products. The two components come in separate tubes, and when they are mixed, a chemical reaction begins which gives the bond its strength and durability. Mix up only as much as you can use immediately. Most epoxies have setting times of less than an hour, and some set in minutes. Because of their thick consistency, they are quite good for filling gaps. Any excess adhesive that squeezes out of the joint can be wiped away with solvent.

The one drawback with this type of adhesive is its cost which is high enough to rule out using it on larger-scale projects. It is best used for jobs where high strength and durability are essential.

White glue (pva adhesive)

These adhesives, which look like white paint, have almost completely taken over as the woodworker's general-purpose glue. They are easy to apply, last for a long time even once opened, set in about thirty minutes and do not stain the wood. As they are water-based, excess adhesive can be wiped off with a damp cloth. The bonds are not waterproof, but resist damp fairly well, and are strong enough for most purposes. The only small drawback is that the adhesive must never be allowed to freeze in its container. It will coagulate, and cannot be used thereafter. So don't keep it in a cold workshop.

Resin adhesives
Resin adhesives are available in two forms, both are two-part adhesives like the epoxy type. One form is a powder with the two ingredients ready-mixed. The addition of water initiates the chemical reaction that makes the adhesive set. The other form has separate components, often in syrup or liquid form, which are mixed and sometimes diluted to start the reaction.

The bond formed with these adhesives is very strong, and is also heat and water resistant. It sets in about three hours. Since the adhesive is nearly as strong as an epoxy and is considerably cheaper, it is used for larger scale projects, particularly when they will be used out of doors.

Nails
The nail is another very old wood fixing device. It was used by the Egyptians, and has been around in various shapes and materials for centuries. Early nails were usually square-cut and tapered to a fairly blunt point, and only the advent of wire drawing machinery made possible the mass-production of the many nails we know today.

One of the most widely used nails in woodworking is the wire nail. This is used on most general carpentry and joinery. It has two distinct sections, the head and the shank. It is available in many sizes and with different shaped heads. The shank is circular in cross-section and without a taper. In general, the duller the point of the nail, the less is the danger of it splitting the wood. Sizes run from about $\frac{1}{2}$ in. (12mm) up to 6 in. (150mm).

For rough carpentry, the common flathead nail is used. This is much stronger than the finishing nail as it has a thicker shank and a large flat head for easier driving. It is therefore used on framing work and the like where the appearance of the head is not important. It splits the wood more easily. Sizes run from $2\frac{1}{2}$ in. (63mm) to 6 in. (150mm).

The lost head or casing nail is a round-shanked nail with a small head, intended to be set below the wood surface. It is stronger than the wire nail, and comes in the same sizes.

Cut nails are square nails that provide a very strong join in rough wood, and are often used in structural woodwork for fixing frames and floorboards, for example. Sizes go up to 6 in. (150mm).

Brads or panel pins are round lightweight nails with almost no head used for delicate cabinetwork and for fixing moldings and beadings into place. The heads are usually set below the wood surface. Sizes run from $\frac{1}{2}$ in. (12mm) to 2 in. (50mm). Hardboard nails are similar, but have a diamond-shaped head that can be driven right into the board surface without setting which is useful when you have a lot of pins to drive. Sizes range from $\frac{3}{8}$ in. (9mm) to $1\frac{1}{2}$ in. (38mm).

Roofing or clout nails are large flat-headed nails used for rough fixing of sheet materials to frameworks, usually outdoors. Sizes range from $\frac{1}{2}$ in. (12mm) to 2 in. (50mm).

Tacks come in all sorts of shapes and sizes, and are used mainly in upholstery, for fixing fabric to frameworks. Variants on the tack principle are the chair or upholstery nail, which has a large domed head, and the escutcheon pin, which has a smaller solid round head. Both these are used where the fixing will be seen.

Chisel point nails are a comparatively recent introduction. The shank is barbed so that once driven in it is almost impossible to remove. It is used particularly for fixing plywood to frameworks, and comes in sizes from $\frac{3}{4}$ in. (18mm) up to 3 in. (75mm).

Nailing techniques

Using nails sounds deceptively simple but it requires skill if you want to avoid bruised thumbs and damaged work. First, choose the right type and size of nail for the job. The descriptions of the various types should help you to pick the nail to use. To nail two pieces of wood together, the nail must be long enough to pass through the upper one and well into the lower one, at least as far as the thickness of the upper piece. Select a suitable hammer. Don't use a heavy claw hammer on a brad.

Hold the nail over the fixing point between finger and thumb, and start the nail with a couple of gentle taps, holding the hammer halfway up the handle. When the nail will stand up on its own, shift your grip to the end of the hammer handle and drive the nail home with several firm strokes. If you want to avoid marking the workpiece, stop just short of driving the nail flush, and finish driving it home with a nail set. Always nail the thinner piece of wood to the thicker one, never the other way around.

To avoid splitting the wood, drill pilot holes slightly smaller than the nail you want to drive first. This applies to plywood and chipboard as well as wood. Don't drive nails close together along the same grain line or you will split the wood along that line. Instead, stagger the nails along the work.

Small pins are often awkward to handle. Start them off with the peen of the pin hammer, hold them with pliers or push them through a piece of thin cardboard which you can tear away just before driving the pin home. If you bend the pin, pull it out with pincers or claw hammer rather than continuing to drive it.

Apart from setting nail heads below the surface, you can also hide them by what is known as secret nailing. Use a chisel to lift a sliver of wood where you want to drive the nail. Then drive it, using a punch if necessary so you don't hit the sliver too, and then glue the sliver back in place over the nail head. With tongue-and-groove boards, drive pins through the tongues and then cover the tongue with the groove of the next board.

Buying nails

You usually buy nails according to their length, and by weight, by the pound or fraction of a pound, or by the kilogram and its fractions. Smaller pins, tacks and specialist nails are often sold in small boxes or packages.

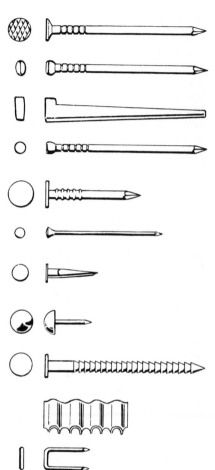

Nails and other fasteners: from the top, round and oval wire nail, cut nail, lost head nail, clout nail, hardboard nail, tack, upholstery nail, chisel point (or annular) nail, corrugated fastener, wire staple

Screws

The screw as a fixing device for woodwork is not recorded until the sixteenth century. Before that the screw bolt threaded into a nut was more common, but both screw and nut had to be made by hand, a very laborious process. In the latter half of the seventeenth century hand-threading machines turned screw making into a thriving industry, stimulated by the introduction of the butt hinge for doors. As these hinges could not be nailed or bolted on, the screw became the standard method of fixing. When machine tools spread to the screw-making industry, mass production became possible, but the screw as we know it today still lacked one vital attribute, a point. Hand-made screws were filed to a sharp point, but the early machines couldn't produce one and the screw could be driven only with the aid of a pilot hole. Automatic machines that could produce pointed screws were patented around 1850, and the modern wood screw was born.

As fixing devices, screws have several advantages over nails. They provide more holding power, they draw the two parts of the work together more tightly than a nail does, they are neater in appearance when properly driven, and they can be removed easily without damaging the material. Against these points must be set the disadvantages that they take longer to fix than nails, and they are more expensive.

The common wood screw consists of a head, a round shank and a threaded section which usually extends for about two-thirds of the length of the screw. The head may be one of several different shapes. The most widely used is the countersunk or flat-head screw, the head of which is designed to be driven slightly below, or flush with the surface of the work. The round-headed screw is used to hold fittings that have not been drilled with countersunk holes, usually metal-to-wood fixings. Hinges are an exception; they are always fitted with countersunk screws. Raised or oval head screws have both a countersink and a domed appearance and are used to fix hardware to wood where the head will be visible and where the item to be fixed has a countersunk hole drilled in it. You may also find heavy-duty screws with a square or a hexagonal-shaped head. These are called lag screws, and have to be driven with a wrench. They are used only on heavy construction work. For decorative work you can buy screws with a domed head. These are basically countersunk screws with a thread drilled in the head to accept the decorative screw-in dome. They are used for fixing panels and mirrors.

The head of all screws is slotted to accept the blade of a screwdriver. This slot is usually a simple cut across the head of the screw, but recent innovations in slot design have led to the Phillips and Pozidriv slots. These are cross-shaped and are driven with a cross-

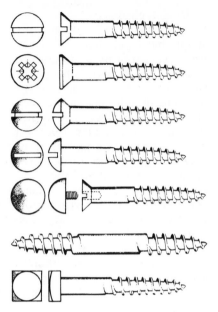

Screw types: from the top, slotted head countersunk screw, Pozidriv countersunk screw, raised or oval-head screw, round-head screw, mirror screw, dowel screw (page 95), lag (or coach) screw

pointed screwdriver instead of the usual straight-bladed one. Both these types are easier to drive accurately, since the tip of the screwdriver engages positively in the head of the screw instead of tending to slip out to the side, as the flat-bladed screwdriver does from a conventional slot.

The shank of the screw is designed to pass through whatever is being fixed, allowing the thread to bite into the surface beneath. The shank diameter is used to indicate the size of the screw, and this is expressed as a number, called the screw gauge, rather than as an exact measurement. These gauge numbers run from 0, equal to $\frac{1}{16}$ in. (1.5mm), up to 20, equal to nearly $\frac{1}{2}$in. (12mm). Most woodworking is done with screws of gauge numbers 4 to 14.

The thread of the screw is its most vital part. Ordinary screw threads consist of a single spiral running from the point of the screw. You can also buy screws with twin parallel threads and two starting points at the tip. These are quicker to drive than conventional screws. They also grip the wood more firmly, and for this reason are widely used when working with man-made boards, especially chipboard, which holds screws poorly. Screws intended for this purpose are often threaded all the way up to the screw head.

Screwdriving techniques

As with nails, you should use a screw at least twice as long as the wood you are fixing. If you are joining sheets use a screw about $\frac{1}{8}$ in. (3mm) less than the combined sheet thicknesses. Because of the relatively large diameter of even a small screw, you can't expect to drive it straight into the surface. Even if you are strong enough to drive the screw in this way and the screw is strong enough not to break, you will certainly split the wood by doing so. It is necessary to drill holes in the wood just a little smaller than the screw diameter, so that the shank and the middle of the threaded part can enter the wood unhindered, while the threads themselves cut into the sides of the hole and provide a positive grip on the wood. Actually it is more complicated than that, since you must drill two holes, one in the wood you are fixing that is about the same size as the screw shank called the clearance hole, and one in the wood you are fixing it to that is slightly smaller than the diameter of the threaded part of the screw called the pilot hole.

Position the two pieces of wood over each other, and clamp them to your bench. Then drill the pilot hole at the fixing position through both pieces, using a depth stop so that the depth of the hole is just less than the length of screw you are using. For small screws you can use a bradawl in softwood. Now drill the larger clearance hole through just the upper piece of wood, using

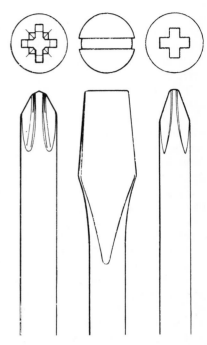

Three types of screw head, with their respective screwdriver tips: Pozidriv (left), slotted (center) and Phillips (right)

the pilot hole as a guide. Finally, use a countersinking bit to form a recess if you are using a counter-sunk screw, and you are ready to drive the screw in.

To save changing drill bits throughout a screwing job, you can use combination screw sets which drill pilot, clearance and countersink holes in one operation.

As you drive the screw in, hold the blade vertical and use the non-driving hand to steady the blade in the slot. Make sure that you are using a screwdriver of the correct size for the screw. If it is too small it will slip in the slot and damage the screw head or slip out and score the work. If it is too large it will not grip correctly, again risking a slip and damaged work, and you will not be able to drive the screw flush with the surface without cutting into it with the edges of the blade. Lubricate the screw threads with wax or soap to ease the driving on hardwoods, and if you are using a soft screw made of brass, for example, drive in a steel screw first to cut the thread. This will prevent the softer screw from breaking as you drive it.

Screws do not hold well in end grain, so if you have to screw into it always dip the screw thread in woodworking adhesive first or drill a hole, insert a fiber or plastic wall plug and screw into that. Or you can drill a hole across one end grain, insert a length of glued dowel into the hole, and then drive the screw into the end grain so it passes through the dowel.

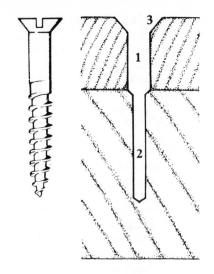

To drive screws successfully, you must first drill a clearance hole, 1. to accept the screw shank, a pilot hole, 2. to take the screw thread and a countersunk hole, 3. for the screw head itself

Pilot and Clearance Holes

Screw gauge	Clearance Hole	Pilot hole (softwood)	Pilot hole (hardwood)
No. 4	$\frac{1}{8}$ in. (3mm)	bradawl	$\frac{5}{64}$ in. (2mm)
No. 6	$\frac{5}{32}$ in. (4mm)	bradawl	$\frac{3}{32}$ in. (2.5mm)
No. 8	$\frac{3}{16}$ in. (5mm)	$\frac{5}{64}$ in. (2mm)	$\frac{1}{8}$ in. (3mm)
No. 10	$\frac{7}{32}$ in. (5.5mm)	$\frac{3}{32}$ in. (2.5mm)	$\frac{9}{64}$ in. (3.5mm)
No. 12	$\frac{1}{4}$ in. (6mm)	$\frac{1}{8}$ in. (3mm)	$\frac{5}{32}$ in. (4mm)
No. 14	$\frac{9}{32}$ in. (7mm)	$\frac{5}{32}$ in. (4mm)	$\frac{3}{16}$ in. (5mm)

Screw finishes

Common wood screws are made of mild steel, which is strong and suitable for most jobs. However, they do rust, and if appearance is important you may prefer screws with another, more decorative finish. Brass screws are always used with oak, which is acidic and corrodes steel screws. Use these also for fitting brass hardware. Aluminum alloy screws are used with aluminum fittings.

You can also buy screws with a steel core and a wide range of finishes. Bright plated screws, finished in brass, chrome, nickel or zinc are used for indoor work where the head will be visible. Antique finishes such as bronze, japanned and copper are used to match or contrast with fittings made in these materials.

In addition to using screws with a decorative finish, you can enhance the appearance of the fixing by using a screw cup or socket. The screw cup is a raised collar which looks attractive and which enables you to fix thin materials that would be weakened by countersinking. Sockets allow the screw head to lie flush with the wood surface, and also make dismantling easier if this is necessary.

Remember that steel screws will rust if you paint over them with water-based paint or fill recessed heads with a water-based filler. To stop this from happening, spot-prime their heads with rust-inhibiting metal primer before you apply the paint or filler.

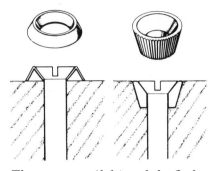

The screw cup (left) and the flush fitting screw socket
Below: an array of screw types and finishes

Buying screws

Unlike nails, screws are bought by number. If you can afford it, buy the sizes you use most often in boxes of 100 or more. They are less expensive bought in larger quantities and a few large boxes will last you longer.

There are several things you must specify when you buy screws. Apart from number, you need to know the length, head type, gauge number, material or finish and slot type in order to get the exact screw type you want.

Fixing to walls and hollow surfaces

If you are faced with fixing wood to walls, or building furniture into an alcove, for example, you can't just bang in a nail. Walls are too hard for one to penetrate; you will need special masonry fixings.

Masonry nails are specially toughened so you can drive them through a wooden batten into the wall beneath. Drill a pilot hole through the wood so it does not split, and then drive the nail in with firm blows of a heavy hammer. The nail should be long enough for at least 1½ in. (38mm) to penetrate the masonry under any plaster. Wear protective goggles when driving these nails, just in case you break one and the bits fly off. Masonry nails are quite brittle, and cannot be straightened if they bend.

If you want to use screws to make your fixing, it's necessary to drill into the wall first with a masonry bit in your power drill, and then insert a plastic or fiber wall plug into which the screw can be driven. Drill clearance and countersink holes in the wood first.

For firmer fixings of heavy-weight wood, use a masonry bolt instead. This has a metal sleeve that fits in the hole drilled in the wall; it expands as you do up the bolt and grips the sides of the hole securely.

For fixings to hollow walls and doors, there is a wide range of cavity fixings—toggle bolts, expanding anchors and collapsible collars, all of which hold the screw and also bear against the back surface of the panel to provide a fixing. If you need to be able to remove them again, use a type with a sleeve that passes through the panel to hold it in place. With most of the toggle types you lose the toggle inside the cavity if you withdraw the screw.

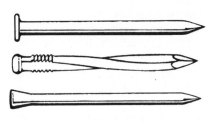

Heavy-duty masonry nail, twist drive nail for lightweight blocks and light duty masonry pin.

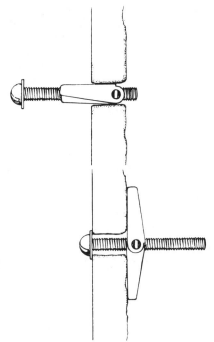

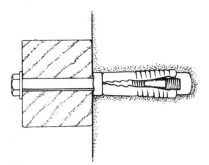

For heavyweight fixings to solid walls, use a masonry bolt. The sleeve expands to grip the sides of the hole securely

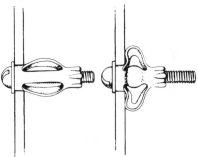

Collapsible collars bear against the inner face of hollow walls as the screw is tightened, and stay in place if it is removed

Spring toggles are easy to fit, but the toggle is lost inside the cavity and cannot be reused if the machine screw is removed

Other fasteners for wood and sheet materials

Although adhesives, nails and screws are the woodworker's standard fixing devices, there are several others available for jobs for which these are not suited.

Nuts and bolts are an example of this. They are usually used in the construction of frameworks that may need dismantling again. The coach bolt has a round head and a square collar that locks into the wood, so that it can be tightened just by turning the nut with a wrench. Hexagonal-head bolts with hexagon nuts may also be used for the same sort of fixing. With both types a washer should be used under the nut and under the head of a hexagonal-head bolt to increase the holding power and prevent the nut or bolt head from cutting into the wood.

Corrugated fasteners are sometimes used on rough work to reinforce butt joints. They are available in depths of $\frac{1}{4}$, $\frac{1}{2}$ or 1 inch (6, 12, 25mm). The flutes taper slightly toward the sharpened end of the fastener, so that when it is driven in across the joint with a hammer it pulls the two parts together tightly. They are almost impossible to remove once they are in place.

Staples, bent wire sharpened at each end, provide a quick way of fastening panels and thin laths. Light-duty staples, similar to those used in offices to bind papers together, are handy for many small fixing jobs, especially upholstery work, and can be fired one-handed from spring-loaded staple guns.

Knock-down corner joints of various patterns are a quick and easy way of joining panels together in frameless furniture. For this reason they are widely used in the manufacture of pack-flat furniture such as kitchen units, and can save a great deal of time in assembling simple furniture. The basic principle on which they work is the same, even if the precise shape varies from manufacturer to manufacturer. The joint usually consists of two plastic blocks. One is screwed to one component of the joint and the other to the second component so that when the two are brought together they meet in a right angle. A machine screw is then driven into a pre-threaded hole to lock the two parts together and complete the joint. Dismantling is easy. Simply remove the machine screw again, and tap the two panels apart. However, precise positioning of the two plastic blocks is essential if you are to get a perfectly-aligned joint. You usually need two pairs of blocks to each joint to make it rigid.

You can also join panels at right angles or edge to edge with metal plates of various shapes. These have pre-drilled screw holes usually with countersinks, and are used where appearance is not important. Another type has holes in one face of the plate and angled slots on the other. This is called a shrinkage plate. You fix the face with the holes to one component, and then bring up the other panel, adjusting its position slightly as you drive round-headed screws into it through the slots at right angles to the grain direction so that you achieve a tight-fitting joint that allows some movement of the wood when it shrinks or expands.

The table plate enables you to reinforce the three-way joint between the leg of a piece of furniture and the two side rails running into it. The plate fits across the inside corner of the joint, with its ends biting into slots on the inside of the rails. A bolt is centered through the leg at an angle of 45°, and protrudes through a hole in the table plate, to which it is tightened by a wing nut.

The leg plate allows simple fixing of legs to tables and similar pieces of furniture. It consists of a plate and a threaded screw. The plate is screwed to the underside of the table top and the threaded screw is wound into the end of the leg. Then the leg is simply screwed into the plate to complete the fixing.

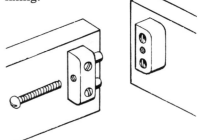

The two halves of knock-down corner joints are pulled tightly together by a machine screw

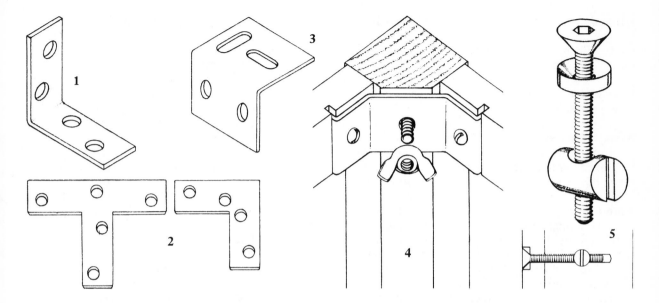

The threaded screw used in this fitting is called a dowel screw and can also come in handy for other jobs where you want to join two pieces of wood end-to-end, a staircase handrail is a good example. Drill a pilot hole in the end of each piece of wood to be joined, and then wind one end of the screw into the hole with pliers. Then the other piece is screwed onto the other threaded end of the screw. Note that this type has a woodscrew at each end. The type used in the table plate has a woodscrew at one end and a machine screw, on which a nut can be threaded, at the other.

Dowels and wooden pegs are also widely used for joints of this sort, but as they need careful marking out and drilling and can be fitted in so many different ways

they are covered in the next chapter.

A whole range of ingenious fittings are made for use in the chipboard furniture industry. You will probably find some on any piece of manufactured furniture bought recently. Some of these are now finding their way onto the do-it-yourself market, and may be worth experimenting with if you are planning to make a lot of panel furniture of this type.

1. right-angled metal plate, useful for joining panels or for fixing wood framework uprights to walls and ceilings; 2. metal repair plates are used to make or repair T- and L-shaped joints; 3. shrinkage plates have angled slots in one face to allow some movement in the wood; 4. table plate, ideal for strengthening corner joints with rails; 5. one of the many ingenious fixings used to make chipboard furniture

Hinges
Hinges are really just moving joints. There is a wide range of types. Here are some of them.

Butt hinge
The simplest of all is the plain butt hinge, used on room and cupboard doors. It consists of two leaves which are recessed into the parts to be linked, and comes in a wide range of sizes.

Piano or continuous hinge
The piano hinge is just a very long butt hinge, used as its name implies to hinge the lids of pianos and any other flap or door that needs support right along its length. It can be bought in long lengths and cut off to the size you need.

Lift-off hinge
The lift-off hinge consists of one leaf with a hinge pin fixed into it, and a second leaf into which the pin fits when the two are joined. The part with the pin is usually fixed to the door, the other to the door jamb, so that the door can be lifted into place and the pins dropped into their sockets. Another type resembles the ordinary butt hinge but has a removable pin.

Rising butt hinge
The rising butt hinge is a lift-off hinge with each part accurately machined so that as the door is opened they ride over each other and raise the door slightly. They are used for room doors that would not otherwise clear carpets.

Flush hinge
Flush hinges are lightweight hinges working in the same way as a butt hinge, but because one leaf fits into a cut-out in the other no recesses are needed. They are useful for fitting hinges to small pieces of furniture where the depth of the recess might weaken thin wood too much.

Concealed hinges
For cupboard doors, an ingenious range of concealed hinges has been designed to allow doors to open within the cupboard's width. The barrel section of the hinge is recessed into the door, and the hinge section is adjustable so that a row of doors can be accurately aligned with each other.

Backflap and table hinges
For table tops and drop-down flaps, you can use special hinges called backflap hinges and table hinges. The former are really wide butt hinges, designed so that the fixing screws are further from the weak edge of the wood. The latter have one flap wider than the other to span the gap left when the flap is lowered.

Most ordinary hinges are made of steel and should be painted if they are not to rust, but you can also buy hinges in solid brass, and with various plated finishes. There is also a wide range of face-fitting hinges in black iron for reproduction work. Fit brass and black iron hinges with screws in the matching finish.

Fitting a recessed hinge
Apart from certain specialized hinges, and those fixed directly to the face of the wood, a shaped recess to house each leaf is needed for the hinge to function properly. This matches the shape of the leaf in outline, and the thickness of the leaf in depth. This is how to fit a simple butt hinge. The principle is the same for other recessed hinges.

Once the hinge position has been chosen the first step is to draw around the outline of the hinge on both door and jamb. The hinged knuckle must lie just clear of the edge of the wood for the hinge to operate smoothly. Also mark the thickness of both hinge leaves on the face of the wood, down from the fixing edges.

Cut around the outline of the recess with a sharp chisel, holding it vertically with the bevel edge facing the waste area. Now with the bevel edge downward, start to clean out the recess with a series of shallow angled cuts, being careful not to cut below the depth line. Cut these out and trim up the recess with the chisel horizontal, bevel uppermost, and place the hinge leaf in the recess to check its size and depth. If it is too small, chisel away more wood until you get it right. If it is too deep, pack it with thin cardboard. Repeat for the other recess.

Finally, make pilot holes through the screw holes, and attach the hinge, aligning the screw heads for neatness. Repeat the process to attach the other leaf.

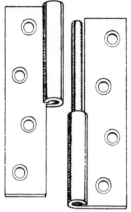

Lift-off hinge

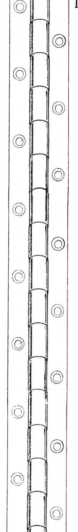

Piano or continuous hinge

Concealed hinge

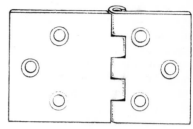

Table hinge

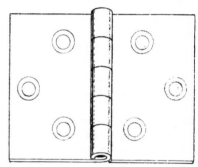

Backflap hinge

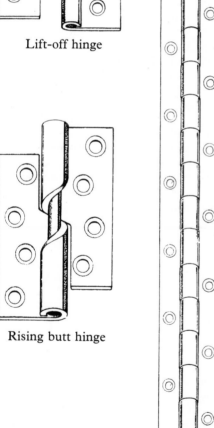

Rising butt hinge

Folded butt hinge

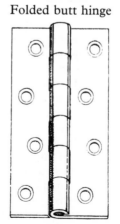

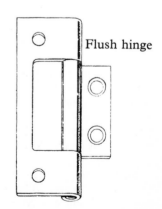

Flush hinge

CHAPTER 7
Woodworking joints

We are so used to reaching for glues, screws and nails to fix wood together, that we forget how efficient and readily available they are. But this was not always the case. Adhesives once had to be made up from raw materials instead of being poured out of a bottle or squeezed from a tube, screws and nails were laboriously made by hand until machines took over the job. So the woodworker devised ways of holding his wood together using just the raw material—the wood itself. He created joints that increased the length and width of wood and found methods of making two pieces of wood interlock so that any stress on the joint increases it holding power. Usually these joints were reinforced with glue and woodworkers soon discovered that by increasing the surface area between the two components, the joint strength is increased too. Gradually the basic joint shapes were refined for the sake of easy cutting and attractive appearance. Today, there are literally hundreds of woodworking joints to do various jobs and create different effects.

Overlap or plain joints are the simplest joints of all. Two pieces of wood to be joined are just laid over each other and glued and nailed or fixed with screws. This joint is used mainly on rough or temporary work.

Butt joints are formed by butting together the pieces to be joined in the same plane instead of one on top of the other as with overlap joints. Nails, screws, glue or other form of reinforcement such as dowel pegs hold the two parts together, so it is important that the meeting surfaces are flat and meet squarely. Butt joints can be used in frameworks and box constructions and for joining angled or mitered components.

Lapped joints have part of one piece of wood cut away so that the whole of the second piece can fit into the cut-out. They are used where one component has a smaller cross section than the other, for example where a rail is notched into a board to form the front and side of a chest of drawers.

Halving joints are similar to lapped joints, but here a cut-out is made in both pieces of wood so that the two halves match perfectly when the joint is assembled. It is widely used in frame constructions.

Housing or dado joints involve cutting a slot in one piece of wood to house the other piece. They are used mainly in the construction of shelving and cabinets.

Rabbeted (rebated) or grooved joints are formed when a groove, called a rabbet in woodworking, is made along the edge of one component and the other component, which may also be grooved with a step shaped cut-out, is fitted into it. Joints of this type are often used in box constructions to increase the gluing area of the joint.

Mortise and tenon joints are among the oldest and best-known woodworking joints. A tenon or tongue is cut on the end of one piece of wood and this is fitted into a matching mortise or slot cut in the piece to be joined. It is the strongest joint for frame constructions and used in making chairs, tables, doors and windows. There are several varieties of mortise and tenon joint for specific jobs.

Dovetail joints are the most complicated joints in everyday woodworking. Dovetail shaped pins are cut in the end of one piece of wood and these fit into matching cut-outs in the piece to be joined so as to resist any stress on the joint. They are used mainly for box type constructions such as in drawers.

Making all of these joints involves a number of common operations which are explained in detail on pages 101 and 103. But before you can start cutting joints, you will have to do some preliminary work on the wood you are going to use. This is called trueing up.

Trueing up

Wood bought ready-planed will be approximately square. In other words, its faces will be roughly at right angles to its edges. But it may have become warped along the length, or cupped across the width by moisture changes since it was planed up. This may not matter on rough work where accuracy isn't essential, but for finer work and perfect joints, you must true up the wood first. It is essential to produce a piece of wood that is perfectly straight and flat in length and width and with edges that are parallel to each other and exactly at right angles to the faces if you are to produce really good joints.

Start by inspecting the wood to decide which of the two wider surfaces, called the faces, is the better. You can gauge the straightness of the board by holding the wood up to your eye and sighting along it. Choose the face with the more attractive grain pattern. The side you choose is called the face side.

1. Place the face side up on the bench or in the vise and plane it flat, taking off as little wood as possible but at the same time being sure that the surface is smooth and even. 2. Check that it's flat across the width with a try square. 3. Check the flatness along the length with a steel straight edge. 4. Test for warp using winding strips. These are thin, narrow battens which are placed across the wood, one at each end. If you sight across them, the misalignment of the far

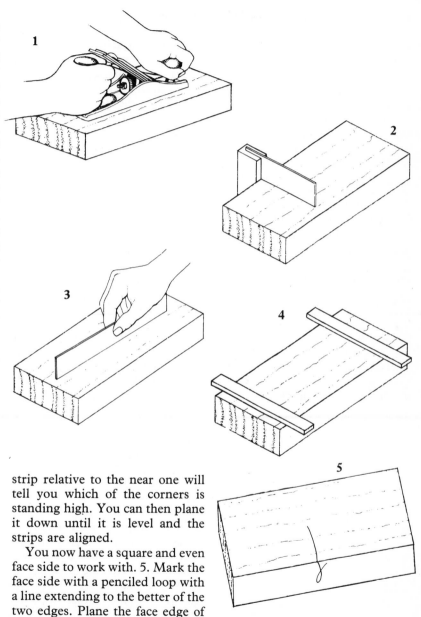

strip relative to the near one will tell you which of the corners is standing high. You can then plane it down until it is level and the strips are aligned.

You now have a square and even face side to work with. 5. Mark the face side with a penciled loop with a line extending to the better of the two edges. Plane the face edge of the workpiece until it is flat and straight and square with the face side. Check for square with a try square, and then mark it as the face edge by continuing your pencil mark into it. All subsequent measurements will be made from these two trued up surfaces.

6. First use the marking gauge to mark the width the wood is to be by running it against the face edge. Saw then plane the edge down to the marked line, which should extend right around the wood, and check the edge for flatness and square to the face side. Then finish up by gauging the wood's thickness, running the gauge against the face side and plane it down as before. Finally check again for flatness and squareness.

The end product of this procedure is a piece of wood exactly the width and thickness that you require which is straight, flat and perfectly square all around. It is ready to be marked out to length and for use in making joints.

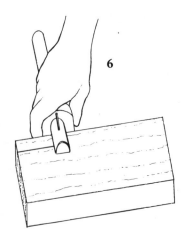

6

Cutting joints

With every joint you cut, you need to follow a sequence of operations to get perfect results. To begin with, the ends of the pieces you are joining must be square. Use the try square with the stock held against the face edge of the wood and mark a line across the wood with the marking knife. Continue this line around the other three sides of the wood using the square and knife. If the fourth line doesn't meet the first one, you have either marked the lines carelessly or the wood isn't square. Check and correct as necessary. Then cut off the waste with the tenon saw, making sure you saw on the waste side of the line. You can now assemble and complete an overlap or a butt joint with the square end you have cut aligned with the straight edge of the other component of the joint. For other types of joint, you have to mark up the parts you are going to remove to make the joint.

The most important thing to remember throughout is that you should always use the dimensions of the two pieces of wood you are joining to do the marking. Often you will be able to use the wood itself to mark the extent of the cut-out on the other piece, especially for the width of the cut-out. For the depth it is more common and more accurate to use a marking gauge set to match the thickness of the wood that the cut-out will receive. To see these steps in action, here is how to go about marking up the two components of

a mortise and tenon joint.

Place the piece of wood in which the mortise will be cut (piece A) in your vise, and lay the other piece (B) over it. Check that B is square to A using the try square and that the point at which you will mark the mortise is the correct distance from the end of A. 1. Then mark the width of B on the edge of A with the marking knife. 2. Use a square to transfer the outline to the opposite edge of A.

3. Now lay B on the bench, face side up, and place A across it so you can mark A's width on B. This will give you the shoulder line for cutting the tenon on B. 4. Square this line around B with the try square. Next select a chisel with a blade width as near as possible to one third the thickness of A. 5. Set the pins on the mortise gauge to match the chisel width. Adjust the position of the stock so that the pin marks are made in the same place on the edge of A whichever side of A the stock is pressed against. This ensures that the marks are central on the edge. 6. Lock the stock position on the stem and mark the outline of the mortise on both edges of A and of the tenon on both edges of B. 7. Hatch in waste areas with a pencil and check that everything is accurately marked before beginning to cut the joint.

The principles are similar when you are marking up other joints. On a halving joint, for example, you mark half of each piece for removal as waste using the marking gauge to mark the depth of the cut-

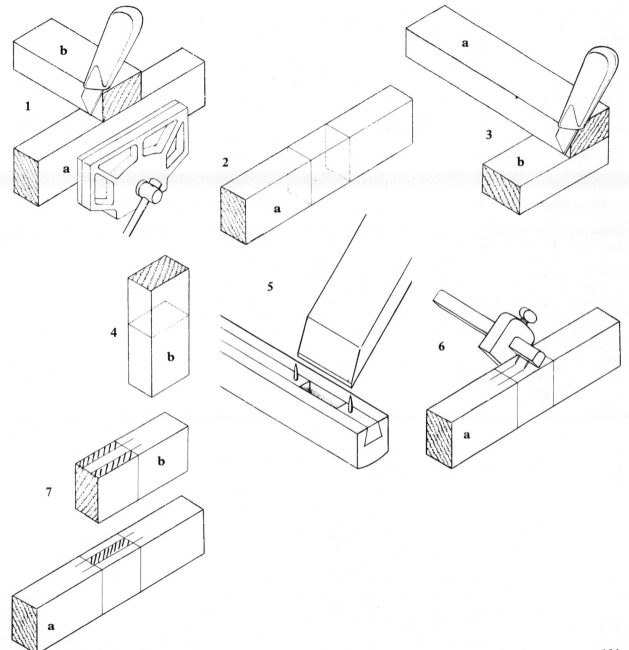

out and the wood itself to mark the width. On a housing joint, the groove depth is marked with a marking gauge and is usually a maximum of one third the thickness of the piece in which it is cut. On a rabbeted joint, a maximum of two thirds of the thickness of the rabbeted piece is marked for removal. Marking miter, dowel and dovetail joints is done with the help of a jig or other aid for accuracy. (see pages 104-105).

The next step is the actual cutting of the joint. Three different processes are called for here according to the shape of the cut-out required. L-shaped cut-outs can usually be made with two saw cuts at right angles. U-shaped cut-outs and grooves are made by sawing down each side of the U and then chiseling along the bottom of the cut-out. An alternative method for deep, narrow U-shapes is to drill a hole at the bottom of the cut-out, saw down to it at each side and then just square up the bottom of the cut-out with a narrow chisel. Finally, slots have to be cut out entirely with a chisel, or with a combination of drilling and chiseling similar to that described for U-shaped cut-outs.

8. To saw away the waste on a tenon, for example, hold the wood upright in the vise and start the cut across the end of the wood. 9. Then tilt the wood in the vise and saw down to the diagonal from each side before leveling the wood again and completing the cut right down to the shoulder line. 10. Then make the cross-cut that completes the cut-out by holding the wood on the bench hook. For both cuts it is vital that you saw just on the waste side of the marked lines. If you don't, the joint will be loose. Take care not to overshoot the depth lines.

On long saw cuts that will form a rabbet or a housing, clamp a batten across the board alongside the marked line to guide the saw cut. Again, be careful not to overshoot the depth lines and to cut within the waste area. Then chisel out the bottom of the cut-out or groove, working from opposite sides toward the middle with the chisel held bevel uppermost.

11. To chisel out a mortise, make a series of angled downward cuts with the chisel, starting at the center of the mortise and working out toward the edge, bringing the chisel up to the vertical as you go. On a through mortise, turn the wood over when you reach about halfway, and cut the rest of the waste out from the other side of the wood. Finish by trimming up the sides of the mortise to make them perfectly square.

12. When you have completed the cutting of both parts of the joint, fit them together to test their fit and make any minor adjustments that may be necessary to ensure an accurate and reasonably tight fit. Clean off any pencil or knife marks, glue the mating surfaces and assemble the joint, clamping it or securing it as appropriate with screws, nails or other fixing devices.

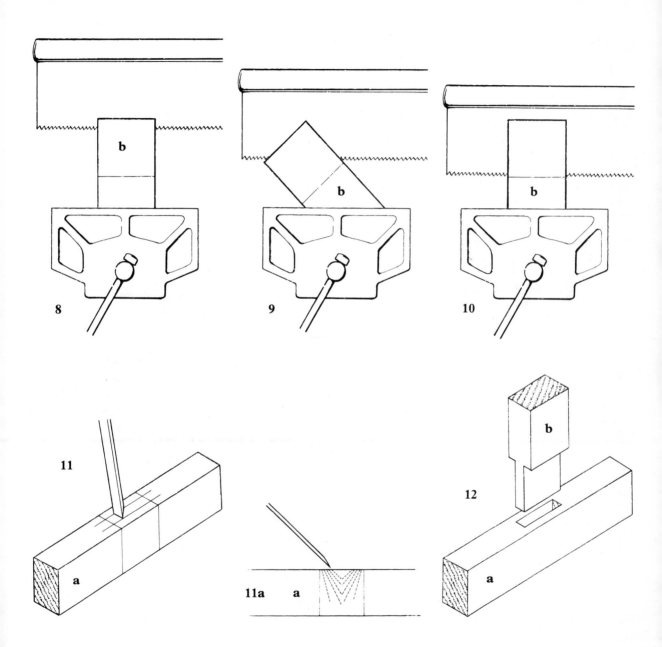

8

9

10

11

11a a

12

Jigs and templates

Three joints you may want to cut involve marking out that cannot be done in the way just described. The first and perhaps the simplest, is the miter joint, where each half of the joint is cut at an angle of 45°. You can use the miter box for cutting miters on small sections, but larger ones have to be marked out for cutting on the bench.

To mark the first component of a miter joint you need either a combination square or a sliding bevel. With the former, you simply hold the stock of the square against the edge of the wood and use the marking knife to mark a line across the wood at the correct angle. Then the wood is held on the bench hook or in a vise as appropriate and the miter is cut carefully with a tenon saw. With the sliding bevel, you have to set the blade at the correct angle to the stock with a protractor. If you don't have either a combination square or a sliding bevel, mark a line square across the wood at the point where the miter will start and then measure the width of the wood and mark this distance on the edge of the wood to create a right angled triangle, the hypotenuse of which will be at 45° to the edge.

When you have cut one component of a miter joint, use it to mark the other one, checking that the two are square to each other as you do so. This will keep the joint square and compensate for any slight inaccuracy in the marking or cutting.

The dovetail joint is trickier to mark out successfully and accurately. To help you, you will need a dovetail template, which gives each pin and tail of the dovetail the correct angle— a slope of 1 in 7. Begin by marking the shoulder lines on both the pieces of wood, adding approximately $\frac{1}{16}$ in. (1.5mm) extra to allow for cleaning up of the edges after the joint is completed. Then mark out the positions of the tails on the shoulder lines and use the template to complete the marking out. Hatch in the waste areas with a pencil.

Now place the wood in the vise, sloping the work so that one set of cutting lines is vertical. Saw down to the shoulder line with a dovetail saw, cutting on the lines rather than within the waste area. Slope the piece the other way to cut the other lines and then use a coping saw or a chisel to cut out the waste between the tails. Make sure that all the cut-outs are level.

Use the tails to mark the positions of the pins on the end down to the shoulder lines and hatch in

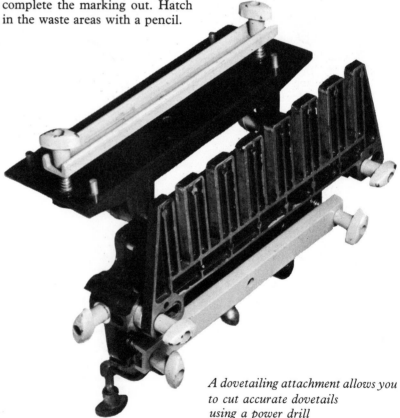

A dovetailing attachment allows you to cut accurate dovetails using a power drill

the waste. Then hold the wood in the vise and cut down the side of each pin with the dovetail saw, working this time on the waste side of the line. Pare away the waste with a chisel and test the joint for fit, making any minor adjustments needed for a tight and accurate fit. Then glue the mating surfaces, assemble the joint and clamp it square. When the glue has set, unclamp the joint and carefully plane off the protruding ends of the pins and tails to complete the joint.

Dowel joints are nothing more than butt joints reinforced with dowel pegs. To make them accurately requires careful marking out and careful drilling of the dowel holes in each component. A doweling jig is an ingenious device that enables you to drill the holes with complete accuracy. All you have to do is mark a center line on each piece to be drilled, clamp the jig over the edge and line up the guides to the spacing you want.

You can also make up a homemade jig for drilling holes of fixed spacing on wood that is all the same thickness by sandwiching a piece of the same wood you will be drilling between two pieces of plywood and making guide holes through the center block through which the dowel holes will be drilled. An alternative way of marking up dowel positions on the wood is to drive small nails or brads into the wood where you want the dowels to go. Then press the other component of the joint onto the pins and pull apart. The nail heads will

A dowelling jig makes it easy to center dowel holes and to drill them precisely vertical

mark the dowel centers on the other component. Pull out the nails, center the drill on the nail holes and drill the holes for the dowel pegs. Use a drill stand and a depth stop to be sure that the holes are drilled precisely vertical and to the correct depth.

Choose a dowel with a diameter no more than half the thickness of the wood to be joined. Cut it to lengths just shorter than required to fill the holes. This prevents the dowel from pushing against the bottom of both holes and stopping the joint from closing. Either saw a groove on one side of the dowel peg

or groove it by pushing it through a homemade grooving block. This is a piece of wood with a hole the size of the dowel drilled in it and a screw driven in through the side of the block so that its tip just enters the hole. Dowel pegs that you cut yourself should be grooved in this way so that excess glue can escape from the hole once the joint is assembled. You can buy ready grooved dowel pegs in a selection of lengths and diameters if you don't want to go through the trouble of making your own.

To assemble the joint, glue one end of the dowel peg and push it into the hole in one component and tap it in lightly. Then glue the other end of the dowel and push the other component onto it using a mallet to close the joint tightly. Wipe away any excess glue that is forced out.

Joint shapes

The Jointmaster

The Jointmaster is a patented device as is the Workmate, and is a jig that can be used for cutting a large variety of joints. By means of a clever arrangement of pegs and saw guides, the workpiece can be held in a variety of angles, ready for operations from a simple right angled cut to more elaborate angled ones. It does nothing that the careful woodworker cannot do with skill and the simpler bench aids, but it is a great confidence builder for the less experienced woodworker. It is sold with complete instructions for its use.

With the Jointmaster, even the beginner can cut accurate joints

Although we have discussed the various types of joint by name, it is far easier to choose a joint according to what you want it to do. Its shape is what matters. If you are making a box, you need a joint for the corners—an L-shaped joint between two boards. If you are making a simple coffee table, you will want a three-way joint where the rails meet the legs. A framework may involve L, T and X-shaped joints. Deciding which type of joint to use and how to cut each one is much easier if you have a visual check list of the various ways each of these joints can be made. On the next pages, you will find joints drawn and described by shape and type. First there are joints between rails, by which we mean sections up to about 1×3 in. (50×75mm). Next are joints with boards, that is wood or sheet materials up to 1 in. (25mm) thick, but considerably wider than 3 inches. Finally, listed are ways of joining rails into boards.

L-joints with rails

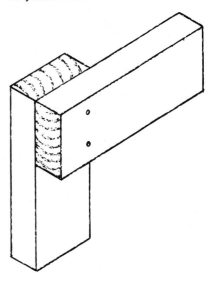

1 SIMPLE OVERLAP JOINT
Formed by overlapping the two rails to form a right angle (as shown) or any other angle for that matter, in which case the angles at the end of each piece would be cut flush after joining. Nails, screws or bolts hold the two rails together. Used only on rough carpentry work.

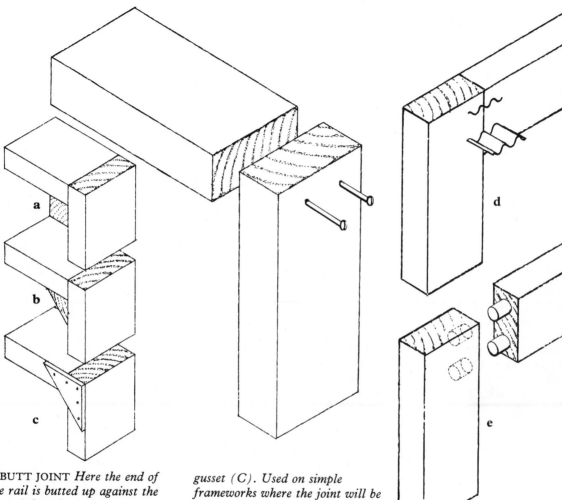

2 BUTT JOINT *Here the end of one rail is butted up against the face of the other, and is secured to it with glue and with nails or screws driven through the face of one rail into the end of the other. It is essential that the cut end is exactly square. The joint is not very strong, and so is often reinforced with a block (A), a triangular fillet (B) or a corner gusset (C). Used on simple frameworks where the joint will be hidden, or where appearance isn't important. When the rails are to be joined on edge, it is not easy to drive a nail or screw through the width of the rail, so corrugated fasteners (D) or dowels (E) are used instead to reinforce the glued joint.*

107

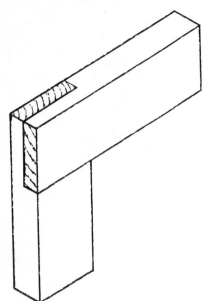

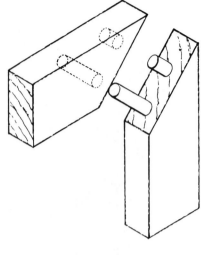

3 HALVING JOINT *Half of each rail is cut away with a tenon saw to form the characteristic halving joint, which is much stronger than the butt joint because of the increased gluing area. It can be reinforced with pins, screws or dowels.*

4 MITER JOINT *This neat joint, with each end cut at 45°, has the advantage of concealing the end grain of each rail. After gluing, it can be reinforced with nails, corrugated fasteners driven across the miter line, or with dowels (as shown). Note that the dowel on the inside of the corner is longer than the outer one.*

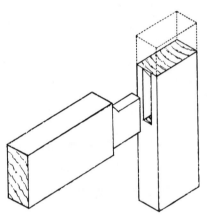

6 HAUNCHED MORTISE AND TENON JOINT *This is the strongest L-joint you can make with rails. The tenon is partly cut away to about two thirds of its full width, and the mortise has one sloping side to match the cut-away. The mortise can pass right through the other rail or can be cut short so the tenon's end grain isn't visible (stopped version). Note that the dotted area of the mortise rail is not cut away until the joint has been assembled and the glue has set.*

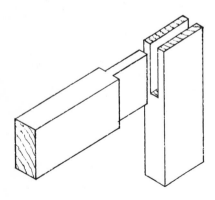

5 BRIDLE JOINT *Stronger than the butt, halving or miter joint, the bridle joint is easy to cut since apart from chiseling out the bottom of the U-shaped cut-out, all the cutting can be done with the tenon saw. Mark it out with a mortise gauge so that the tongues are one third the thickness of the wood. Glue all the matching surfaces, and reinforce the joint with screws or dowels passing through the tongues.*

L-joints with boards

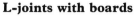

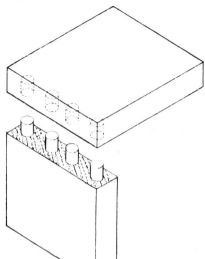

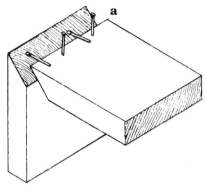

8 MITER JOINT *To conceal end grain or the unattractive core of man-made boards, use a miter joint instead, and reinforce the gluing either with nails driven in at opposing angles (A) or with dowels (B). Cutting accurate*

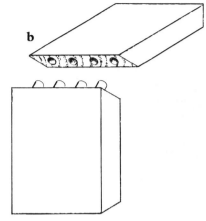

miters across wide boards is a job for a power saw with a tilting sole plate. It's almost impossible to do accurately with a handsaw.

7 BUTT JOINT *Two boards can be joined at a corner in the same ways as two rails—see 2. Such joints can also be made with knock-down corner joints (page 94), or can be reinforced with dowels as shown here.*

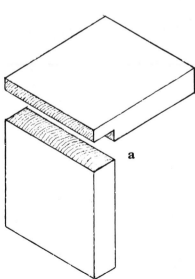

9 RABBETED (REBATED) JOINT *This joint is stronger than a butt joint because the gluing area is greater. It is also more attractive because the end grain is partly concealed. The rabbet can be cut in one board (A), or in both (B), using a tenon saw held against a guide batten for the cut across the grain.*

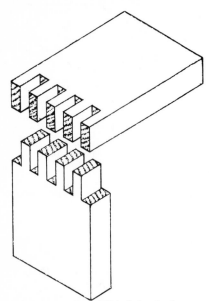

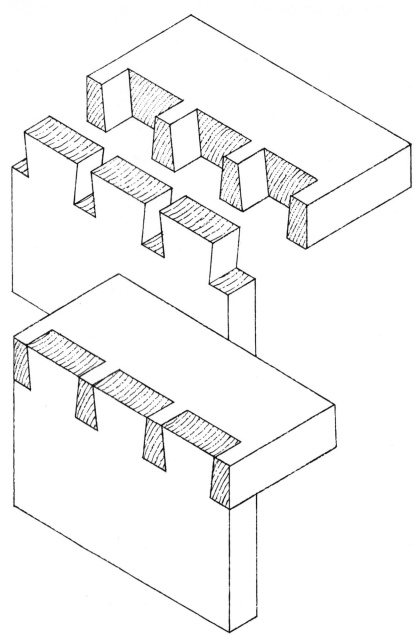

10 BOX JOINT *This joint looks especially neat on box-type constructions. Mark out both pieces of wood in one operation, with the fingers slightly overlong, and cut out the fingers with tenon saw and chisel. Then when the joint is assembled and glued, the finger ends can be planed flush for a neat finish.*

11 DOVETAIL JOINT *This is the joint to use when the construction you are making will be subject to a lot of stress, as in a drawer, for example. Because the pins and tails of the joint are angled, the joint is just pulled tighter if it is strained. It's not as hard to cut as it looks. The secret is in accurate marking out and careful cutting, using tenon saw and bevel edge chisel.*

110

L-joints between rails and boards

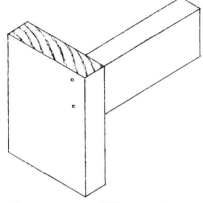

12 BUTT JOINT *When you want to join a rail to a board, for example as a cross rail in a chest of drawers with paneled sides, the simplest way of doing so is with a butt joint, reinforced as before with nails, screws or even corner joints.*

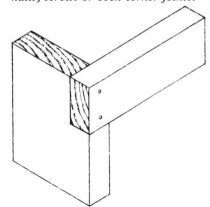

13 FULL LAP JOINT *A stronger alternative to the butt joint is the full lap joint. In solid wood the joint is preferable to a butt joint, since the screws or nails are not being driven into end grain.*

T-joints with rails

14 OVERLAP JOINT *As with L-joints, the simplest T-joint is the plain overlap, reinforced with nails, screws or bolts. As before, the joint angle need not be a right angle, so the joint is useful when making up rough carpentry frameworks.*

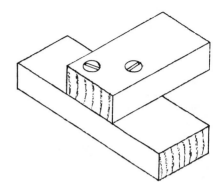

15 BUTT JOINT *Butt T-joints need reinforcing with nails, screws or blocks, and the leg of the T must be cut square. If nailing, drive the nails in at slightly different angles (A). Where you can't get at the top of the T to do this, drive nails at an angle downward through the leg of the T into the other rail. This is called skew nailing (B). Where rails meet on edge, strengthen the joint with dowels (C), or use corrugated fasteners.*

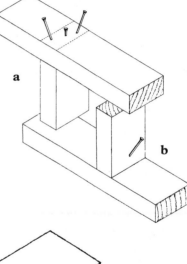

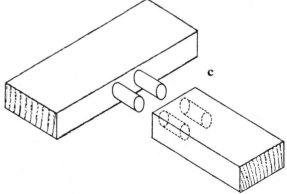

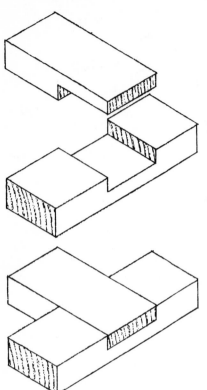

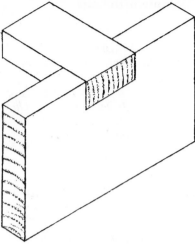

17 FULL LAP JOINT *Where one rail is wider than the other, you can cut a full lap joint instead, making a cut-out with tenon saw and chisel the same size as the smaller rail and securing it with nails or screws. This joint can be used to join a rail and a wider board too, as in 13.*

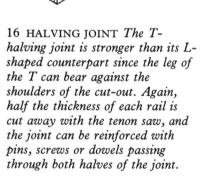

16 HALVING JOINT *The T-halving joint is stronger than its L-shaped counterpart since the leg of the T can bear against the shoulders of the cut-out. Again, half the thickness of each rail is cut away with the tenon saw, and the joint can be reinforced with pins, screws or dowels passing through both halves of the joint.*

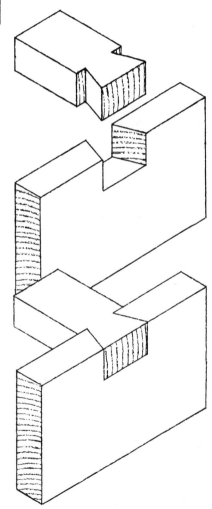

18 SINGLE DOVETAIL JOINT *This is a variation on the full lap joint, and has a dovetail-shaped tongue cut with the tenon saw on one rail and a matching slot cut with saw and chisel in the other. It's a useful joint where there will be a pull on the narrower rail, since in this case the dovetail simply pulls the joint tighter. It can join rails to boards too.*

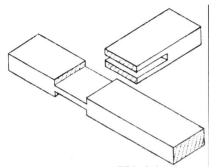

19 BRIDLE JOINT *This joint is stronger than the full lap and halving joints, because the gluing area is greatly increased. Use a mortise gauge to mark it out and a tenon saw and chisels to cut it.*

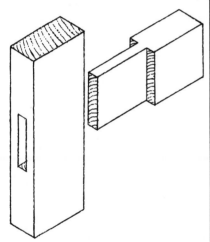

20 MORTISE AND TENON JOINT *As with the L-joints, this type is the strongest T-joint. The mortise can pass right through the wood (as here), or can be stopped—cut only part of the way through with the tenon correspondingly reduced in length so that no end grain shows once the joint is assembled.*

T-joints with boards

BUTT JOINTS *You can make butt T-joints in the same ways as for L-joints, reinforcing the joints with nails or screws or using blocks, fillets, gussets or dowels.*

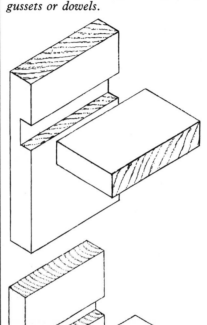

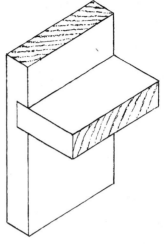

21 HOUSING JOINTS *This is a stronger joint, particularly where the horizontal board will be carrying a load as in a bookcase. The end of one board is housed in a groove cut right across the other board with tenon saw and chisel to a maximum of half its thickness.*

22 STOPPED HOUSING JOINT *Here the groove stops just short of the front edge of the vertical board and the horizontal board is notched correspondingly to fit it. The appearance is that of a butt joint when assembled.*

T-joints between rails and boards

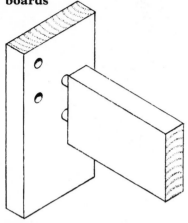

23 BUTT JOINTS *Butt joints are the simplest way of joining these components, with the usual reinforcement of nails, screws, or best of all, dowels. If the dowel holes do not pass right through the board, the join will be neatly concealed.*

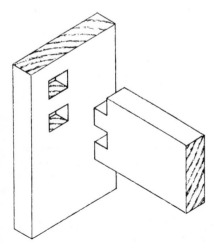

24 BARE-FACED TENON JOINT *Once again, the idea behind this joint is to conceal the fixing so that it looks like a butt joint when assembled. The mortise in the vertical board is stopped so no end grain is visible, while the tenon is really a rabbet cut with the tenon saw in the end of the rail.*

25 STUB TENON JOINT *Another concealed joint, with the stubs fitting into square cut-outs in the vertical board. This joint can be cut equally well with the mortised member horizontal. Its advantage lies in the fact that a number of small mortises do not weaken the board as much as one large mortise would.*

X-joints with rails

26 OVERLAP JOINT *For rough framing work, the simple overlap joint is the easiest to use. It should be reinforced with nails, screws or bolts, and can obviously be made at any angle.*

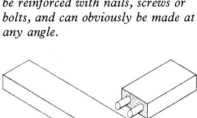

27 BUTT JOINTS *Butt joints can be made in one of two ways—with corrugated fasteners (see 2D) or with dowels. You can either make the doweled joint in two parts, attaching first one side rail and then the other as shown, or you can fit two long dowels through the center rail and attach the side rails to opposite ends of the dowels.*

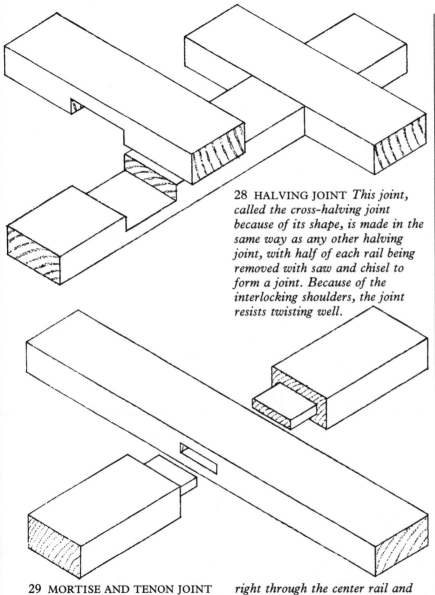

BUTT JOINTS *The only realistic way in which two boards can be butt jointed is with the use of dowels. These should pass right through one board, so that the ends of the two side boards are located on the dowel ends.*

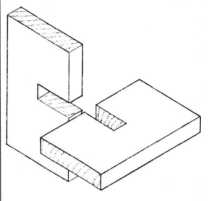

28 HALVING JOINT *This joint, called the cross-halving joint because of its shape, is made in the same way as any other halving joint, with half of each rail being removed with saw and chisel to form a joint. Because of the interlocking shoulders, the joint resists twisting well.*

30 HALVING JOINT *This is the type of joint used on the corrugated dividers of cases of bottles. A slot is cut in each board as wide as the board is thick and reaching to the mid-point of the board. Then the two boards are simply slid together. A tight fit is essential, since it is not easy to glue neatly.*

29 MORTISE AND TENON JOINT *As usual, the mortise and tenon joint provides the strongest way of joining rails. The mortise passes* *right through the center rail and the tenons are cut on each side rail so that they meet in the center of the mortise.*

115

Three-way joints

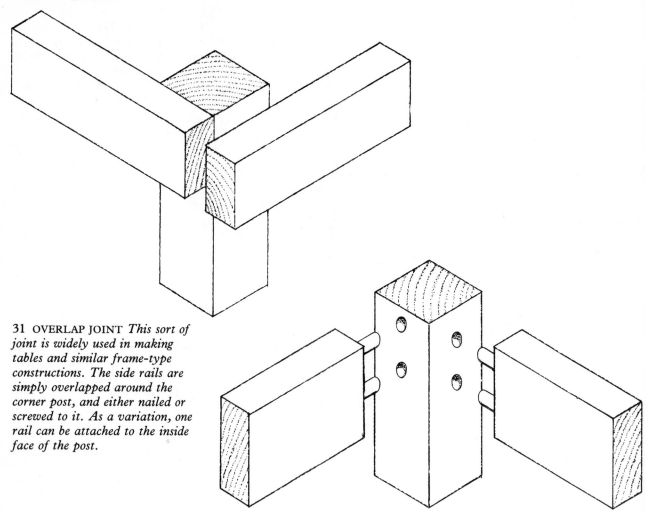

31 OVERLAP JOINT *This sort of joint is widely used in making tables and similar frame-type constructions. The side rails are simply overlapped around the corner post, and either nailed or screwed to it. As a variation, one rail can be attached to the inside face of the post.*

32 BUTT JOINT *The rails can be joined to the corner post as simple butt joints, although some extra reinforcement is always necessary. This can be provided by a block or* *fillet fixed to the interior angle of the corner, or can be provided as here by dowels. Note that the pairs of dowels are staggered so that they miss each other within the post.*

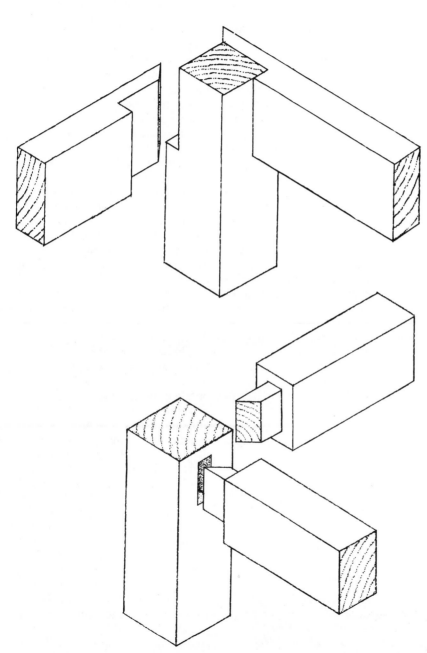

33 LAP JOINT *Alternatively, the rails can be lapped around the top of the post. If the rails are much thinner than the post, a full lap joint can be used, with the post cut away on adjacent sides to accept the full width of the rails. If this could leave a very small stub at the top of the post, use the half lap joint instead, as here. Half of each rail is cut away and corresponding cut-outs are made in the post to accept them. The outside corner of the joint looks neatest if the rail ends are mitered.*

34 MORTISE AND TENON JOINT *This neat, strong joint is more difficult to cut than the other three-way joints, but is much the best choice for a framework that will have to put up with heavy use—on a chair, for example. Note that the tenons are narrower than the rails (alternatively they can be cut as haunched tenons), and that they are mitered to meet in the center of the post. The mortises are chopped through from adjacent faces of the post, and must be carefully cleaned out before the joint is assembled.*

Edge joints

There will be times when you want to assemble a number of narrow boards to create a wide surface instead of using one wide board for the job. This means joining the boards edge to edge, a job that requires careful preparation and accurate assembly. Obviously the edges to be joined must be perfectly straight and absolutely square to the board faces. Otherwise the finished board will undulate. So each edge must be carefully trued up and checked for bowing or warping. It is then used as a guide for the next edge which is planed to fit it exactly so that when the two are placed edge to edge no light can be seen through the join.

The other point you need to remember is that the finished assembly will warp if all the boards are joined with their grain in the same direction. To avoid this the boards should be arranged so that the grain runs alternately up and down on every other board. Remember this as you plane matching edges and number each pair of edges when you've planed them to be sure that you assemble them in the right order.

Boards over about 1 in. (25mm) thick can be joined as simple butt joints, with glue forming the bond. Thinner pieces are difficult to join in this way unless they are tongued and grooved. You can buy boards for paneling with machined tongues and grooves or you can cut them yourself with a milling attachment for the electric drill.

For extra strength, the butt joints can also be doweled at intervals of about 9 in. (225mm). As with other dowel joints, the dowel holes must be accurately drilled.

To be sure that the glued joint is strong and well-made, clamp the boards after assembly with long or sash clamps. Unless you are using dowels, rub the matching surfaces together to force the glue into the wood and then guide them into their final position for clamping. This procedure, called "rubbing" the joint, ensures that all air is expelled from the joint and that the glue will have maximum effect.

Fix the clamps on alternate sides of the assembly to prevent it from buckling and check that the surface across the boards is absolutely flat before clamping it tight and leaving it to set. When the glue has set, remove the clamps, cut the surface to length and finish.

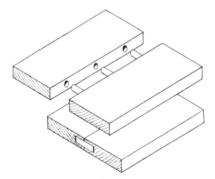

Edge joints should be reinforced with dowels unless the board is more than 1 in. (25mm) thick

Joints with sheet materials

If you are working mostly with sheet materials, you may want to make joints more complex than butt joints. Butt joints are easy to make and assemble particularly if you are using knock-down fixtures, but there are times when a stronger joint will be needed or when you will want to hide the core of the sheet at the ends.

L-shaped corner joints can be mitered, although it is not easy to cut accurate miters across a board without a power saw which can be adjusted to make angled cuts. Rabbeted and grooved joints can be used successfully on plywood and chipboard, although with chipboard you must be careful not to cut too deep a groove or the board will be weakened. With blockboard and laminboard be careful about the exact position of the groove so that you don't cut it on a gap in the core.

T-joints will usually be cut as housing joints, although as with rabbets these must not be cut too deep or they will weaken the board. Cutting through the outer veneers on blockboard and laminboard will, of course have this effect too.

X-joints can be formed only by cutting interlocking slots in each board like the cardboard dividers used in packing crates. The only three-way joint involves the fitting of a bottom or back to a box-type construction. This will usually be a butt joint with the bottom or back panel pinned and glued or screwed to the edges of the other panels. An alternative is for the bottom or back panel to fit in a groove cut near the edges of the side panels. Obviously the bottom or back panel has to be inserted into the groove before the fourth side is added to the box.

Edge joints are possible only with sheets over about $\frac{5}{8}$ in. (15mm) thickness. If thinner boards are to be butt jointed, some form of reinforcement must be provided behind the join to which both panels can be fixed for support.

Choosing the right joint for the job

With so many joints to choose from it is often difficult to know which one to use for a particular purpose. Obviously the shape of the joint will be the first consideration and the material to be joined will be the second. But when you have narrowed the choice down, you will still be left with several options. Here are some general points about the types of joints and the purposes for which they are best suited.

Simple overlap or plain joints are suitable only for the roughest carpentry work. Nail, screw or bolt them together for strength and to prevent twisting.

Butt joints, strengthened with nails, screws, fixing devices or reinforcing brackets are used where the appearance of the joint is not important and where visible end grain in wood or in boards is acceptable. Nailed butt joints can split quite easily during fixing. Avoid this by leaving an extra

length overlapping on the piece through which you are nailing and cut it off when the joint is complete.

Lapped joints are considerably stronger than butt joints although they don't resist stress along the lapped rail very well.

Halving joints give a positive interlock against pushing stresses along each board, but the joint can still tend to pull out if the stress is reversed unless the components are dovetailed together. It shows end grain on both surfaces when used at corners.

Housing or dado joints are the classic way of joining a board end to an upright when it is the board that has to carry a load. By cutting the housing only part way across the upright, the joint is concealed at the front edge.

Rabbeted or rebated joints are useful on box-type constructions where the increased gluing area makes for more strength than a butt joint. Pinning provides extra reinforcement.

Mortise and tenon joints are the strongest of the framing joints and the various types are widely used in furniture work. Remember that the mortise should not be more than one third of the width of the joint and its length should not be more than six times its width. To locate the tenon more firmly in the mortise it can be wedged or held with dowels. Variations include the stopped mortise where the tenon does not go right through the workpiece; the shouldered tenon

which is cut down to slightly less than the rail height to conceal the mortise; the haunched tenon, which is used as an L-joint to avoid overweakening the stile and the double tenon which is used for wide rails where a simple tenon would require too long a mortise.

Dovetail joints are the strongest of board joints and are used particularly where one board is pulled away from the other in use as in a drawer. It is a very decorative joint if it is carefully cut and neatly finished. The lapped dovetail has tails that do not go right through the piece containing the pins, so the end grain on that face of the corner is hidden. You can get a good idea of the right joint to use for a particular job by examining a manufactured specimen of what you want to make, a chair, a table or a bookcase for example. This is particularly true if you look at an older piece of solid wood furniture for which the traditional joints were used.

In the next chapter, the process of choosing and using these joints well be related to the planning and design of the furniture and other projects you will want to make.

CHAPTER 8
Planning

The minute you decide to make something, the idea begins to evolve into an end product. The design process is the stages of development from the idea to the finished piece. If this process follows a logical progression and a few simple rules, the outcome will be successful more often than if your ideas just grow as you work. A few lucky people can build things in this intuitive way, but for most of us, the results of working without planning are usually poor and occasionally disastrous.

The obvious starting point in determining a design is the function of whatever you are planning to make. A bookcase must have shelves set far enough apart to hold your books and be sturdy enough to take the weight. A chair must fit the basic shape of the person who is going to sit in it and should also take into account the way in which it will be used, for example as a dining chair or an easy chair.

Size is the next criterion to consider. For many things, the size will be dictated by normal everyday use and there are standard dimensions for many things. Dining tables are about 30 in. (760mm) high and the seats of dining chairs are about 17 in. (430mm) high. Standard measurements must of course be varied to suit the height and preference of the user. Furniture for children is scaled down in size and a tall person may prefer higher tables. Size will also be determined by the space available for what you are

making and the proportions of the other furniture in the room.

Furniture that is free standing must be firm and secure especially if it will carry weight. Its strength must match the job it will do. Built-in furniture uses the walls for support and sometimes even the ceiling, so the strength of these surfaces will be as important as the strength of the thing you are making. Furniture that will be moved can be fixed on castors for easy movement.

The internal layout and overall structure of a piece has to be planned too. First you must decide whether what you are making will be a simple board construction called a carcass or will be a framework left open or paneled later. Will it have internal partitions, shelves or drawers and where will these go? Rails or dividers to add structural support must also be considered. As each decision is made, you are getting closer to your final design.

Materials are the next vital factor. Will you work in softwood or hardwood, or in sheet materials like plywood or hardboard? How will the work be finished and what sort of hardware is appropriate? These questions will be determined by cost and by the type of piece you are making.

Then there is the all-important question of style. You have to decide between modern furniture and old-fashioned work perhaps with decorative touches. A skilled cabinetmaker is quite capable of

imitating furniture of all styles but the amateur woodworker will be more concerned with matching existing furniture and in increasing his skill in working with wood.

Most modern furniture is quite simple in design with relatively little in the way of decoration. Shape and finish are more important factors and if you aim to match these features with other furniture in your house, you will be at least halfway toward producing a pleasing design. If inspiration or invention is totally lacking, you can always borrow a design. Copying a piece of furniture you like won't be breaking the law as long as you are not planning to go into production and sell the design. At least then you will know what the piece looks like before you start and you will be able to note the joints used in making it and the finish, fixtures and hardware needed to make it. Making a couple of projects in this way could give you all the confidence and experience you need to go on to design and make your own furniture.

Shapes and sizes

The function of what you are making is going to dictate broadly the shape, size and layout you will follow. Here is a summary of some of the commonly accepted and in some cases critical measurements of a number of pieces of everyday furniture. They are intended to give you a starting point from which you can revise measurements up or down to suit your purpose more precisely.

In the kitchen the first crucial measurement is the height of the worktop. This must be matched to the height of the cook and must be high enough to work at comfortably for relatively long periods both standing and sitting. The usual range of heights is from 32 in. (812mm) for a short person to 36 in. (915mm) for a tall person. The worktop depth is usually between 21 and 24 in. (533 and 610mm) which dictates the depth of the cabinet below. It is usual to have an inset plinth at floor level to allow the cook to work close to the sink or worktop. This is between 3 and 6 inches high (75 to 150mm).

Above the work counter there is a gap of at least 20 in. (505mm) to the underside of cabinets on the wall. Kitchen cabinets are usually at least 12 in. (305mm) deep so that they do not overhang the worktop too much while still providing enough depth of storage. The main shelves should be well-spaced to allow tall containers and packages to be stored. The top of the highest shelf should be within easy reach of the outstretched arm unless a stool or ladder is provided in the kitchen for reaching higher shelves. Broom closets must be tall enough for vacuum cleaners, brooms and ironing boards to be put away.

In the living room easy chairs should have a height measured at the front of the seat of about 15 in. (375mm) and a seat depth of about 27 in. (685mm), though these measurements will obviously be varied to suit the seat style and upholstery. Room dividers and shelf units will be tailored around the items they are storing—books, records, hifi equipment, cocktail cabinets and so on, but the main

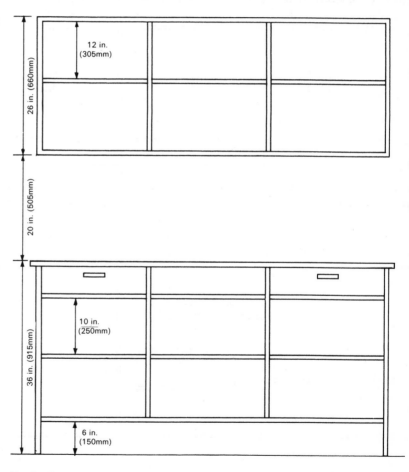

Basic dimensions for kitchen furniture

working or storing surface is usually best at a height of about 28 in. (710mm) above the floor for comfortable and easy access.

Dining tables are generally between 28 and 30 in. (710 to 760mm) high while dining chairs have seat heights around 12 in. (305mm) less to allow for a comfortable sitting position. Sideboards are best with their upper surfaces at the same height as the main surface of living room storage units, that is 28 in. (710mm).

In the bedroom, closets must be at least 24 in. (610mm) deep to allow clothes to be hung without creasing and squashing. Hanging rails are usually fixed at a height of about 5 ft. (1530mm) and the hanging space built to take into account the type and amount of clothes to be hung. Overcoats need about 4 ft. 3 in. (1295mm) in length, dresses up to 4 ft. (1220mm) and suits about 3 ft. (915mm). Top closets should not be more than 6 ft. 3 in. (1905mm) above floor level to allow for easy reaching of bulky items such as

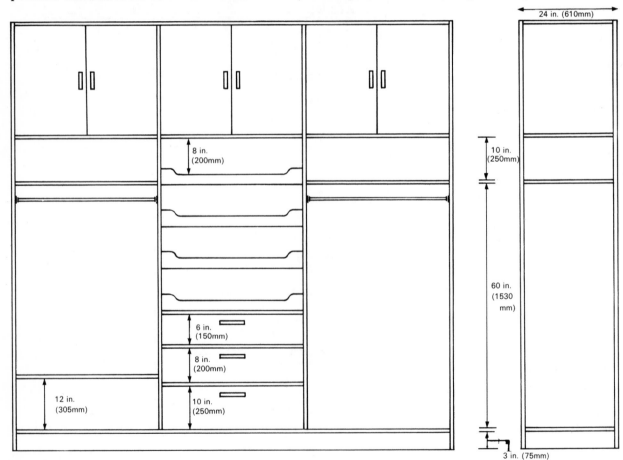

Basic dimensions for bedroom furniture

122

blankets, boxes and suitcases.

Bedside night tables should be a little higher than the top surface of a made up bed. Headboards need to be high enough to give adequate head support—at least 2 ft. (610mm) above pillow level.

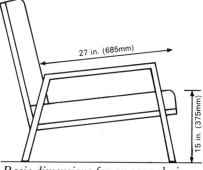

Basic dimensions for an easy chair (above) and a dining table and chair (below)

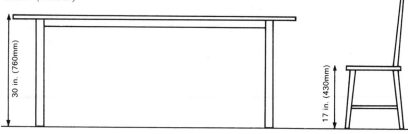

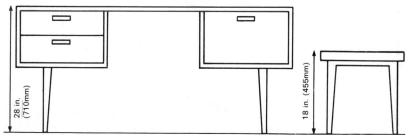

Basic dimensions for dressing table and stool

Dressing tables need to allow enough knee room suggesting an overall height of about 28 in. (710mm) and a kneehole width of about 24 in. (610mm).

All these measurements are intended to be a general guide. Modify them to suit your storage needs and the height of the user as appropriate. Don't hesitate to note down the proportions of a piece of furniture that you see if it has a pleasing design and is comfortable. This applies particularly to chairs, which are difficult to design so that they are good looking and comfortable. The more chairs you try out, the more likely you are to find a combination of seat height and depth that suits you perfectly.

Designing for real

Perhaps the easiest way to see the design process in action is to apply it to a particular project. This will also introduce the subject of working drawings, the blueprints for what you are making. Many woodworkers are reluctant to put pencil to paper, saying that they can't draw and so they try to work without proper working drawings. You don't need to be a draftsman to produce a decent working drawing. All you need is a suitable drawing board or work surface, some good-sized sheets of drawing paper, a couple of fairly soft pencils and one or two elementary drawing instruments such as a ruler, plastic triangle with angles of 90°, 60°, 30° or 45° and a pair of compasses.

If we put the design process to work on a specific project the way in which it works will be clear. The project is to make a small side table for the living room which will support a table lamp and have enough room for a coffee cup or ashtray and also provide room for a bookshelf.

The primary consideration is the overall size of the table. It is intended to be used by someone sitting in an easy chair and will stand alongside the chair within easy reach. A rectangular shape seems sensible. Start by drawing a basic box sketching the chair next to it to see how the two appear side by side. Work with the proportions using a steel tape as a measure so your work isn't approximate and so that you don't plan to make a table

123

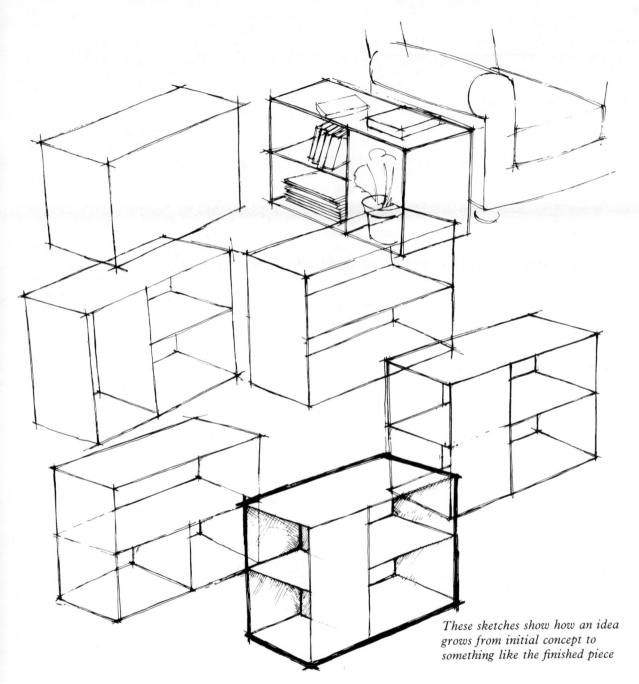

*These sketches show how an idea
grows from initial concept to
something like the finished piece*

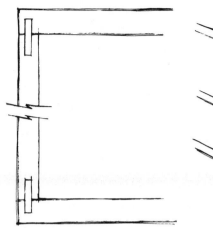

Joint details need attention too. Dowels will strengthen the corners

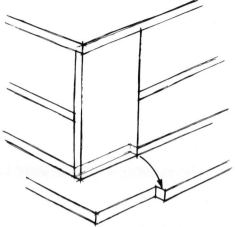

A simple lap joint means a neat finish between side and base

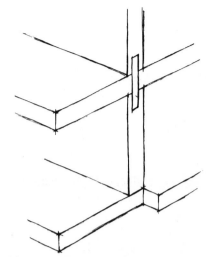

More dowels help keep the central dividers in place

which is either much too big for the room or too small to do its job.

Once you have determined the overall size of the unit, decide how much storage you want it to have. Since it is a sort of coffee table, room for some larger books would be appropriate and you may want to store them lying on their side rather than standing up. You will have to include a shelf wide enough to accommodate their width. Try including the shelf at either end of the unit or try including a divider in it. You will probably want a shelf for smaller books to be stored upright too, so incorporate this into your design. You may find that you have room for a third shelf too. Measure the actual sizes of the books you will store so that you don't make the shelves too close together.

Next you will have to decide how to join the material you are using together. If you sketch the corners and internal connections you can easily choose the kind of joint that is most appropriate from the range on pages 106 to 117. You will have to consider appearance and strength in deciding on the joint to use. Butt joints and simple lap joints seem to be the solution for this design problem as it is a simple and relatively lightweight unit and you will want to make it fairly quickly.

To make the table quickly and not too expensively, you will probably decide to use plywood, blockboard or chipboard and you may want a wood finish to match other furniture in the living room. Veneered plywood and blockboard are quite expensive, so you will

probably choose veneered chipboard which is available in a variety of wood veneer finishes.

If you want to make the table movable, you can fix castors to the bottom. Take this additional height into consideration when you are working out the final dimensions of the table.

Working drawings
When you have reached this stage in the design work, you have to decide on the sort of working drawings you will need to make the unit accurately and correctly. There are no set rules to follow for this, but whatever type you choose, the drawings must include all the relevant measurements and construction details and must be drawn to scale.

Drawing to scale means using a

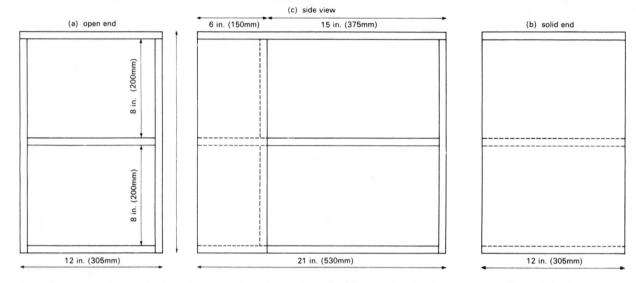

Simple end and side elevations carry all the information needed for a simple piece like this. They show the open end, side view and closed end of the table we've designed, with all the relevant dimensions

small measurement on your drawing to represent a larger one on the actual unit. The scale you choose depends on the size of the unit you are making and on your preference for metric or standard measures. For a project like the side table, a scale of 1 to 4 will be about right and you will produce a sketch about 4 by 6 inches (100 by 150mm). If you are using the metric system, a scale of 1 to 5 will be less confusing as the subdivisions are easier to use. Here a 25mm unit on the actual piece will be represented by 5mm on the drawing.

The simplest drawings you can do are a series of plans, that is the view looking down and elevations, drawings of the sides of the

ture like those drawn for house plans. Here you will need elevations of the side and of each end of the unit. Drawing these requires no knowledge of perspective, just the ability to use a scale accurately and to keep the lines square. Use the set square for this and check that parallel lines are the same length. You will of course have to know the thickness of the materials you are using so that you can allow for this in your calculations. In the side table for example, the height of the sides will be the height of the unit minus the thickness of chipboard. These drawings will be on your workbench as you work so they must have all the information you will need about sizes and joints. Record them accurately

either on the elevations or as details on the border of the drawing so that you have them handy.

For a more complicated construction, you may find that simple plans of this type are not enough. If you have a good eye for perspective drawing, even if it isn't technically accurate you can easily prepare a more carefully drawn version of your rough sketches adding the same details of sizes and joints as before. A perspective drawing is not a scale drawing, however, and you may want to produce an isometric drawing instead as it can be drawn to scale. An isometric drawing combines three views in one drawing. All vertical lines are vertical, and all horizontal lines are drawn so that they are 30° to the

126

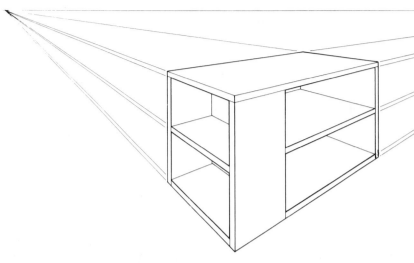

A perspective drawing is not too difficult to produce and gives the only realistic view of how what you have designed will really look. All the lines meet at what are called the vanishing points

horizontal using a 30° triangle. The length of all the lines are drawn to scale as true lengths instead of allowance being made for the effects of perspective. Because of this, and because all the lines are parallel, the drawing may look distorted, but it records all the information you will need in a readily usable form.

Making models

If you find it difficult to visualize things from your working drawings, whether elevations or isometric drawings, you can get a good idea of what you have designed and how it will look in real life by making a simple scale model of it. This is much easier than trying to do a perspective drawing which requires some artistic training if it is to be realistic. Balsa wood is an ideal material for model making and is available in thin sheets or narrow strips to represent man-

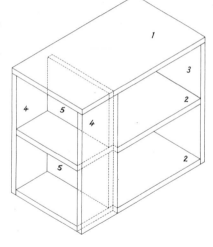

An isometric drawing combines elements of scale and perspective drawings in one, although it does result in a rather distorted image of the piece. Numbering all the parts provides a cross check with the cutting list (overleaf) and helps to avoid errors

made boards or sections of wood. It is easy to cut with a sharp knife and quick to join with balsa cement. You can shape it with a file or fine sandpaper and can pencil features on the surface.

If it is vital that the piece you are making fits exactly in scale with existing furniture and if it is a piece of fine furniture using expensive hardwoods, you may want to construct a life-size model. This is easiest to do for carcass constructions using thin rough-sawn wood to make up a framework the same size as the finished piece and using heavy cardboard to fill in paneled areas. Details like drawers, doors and hardware can be drawn on with pencil or felt-tip pen. You can then carry the complete mock up into the room where the finished piece will be and compare it in proportion to the existing furniture. Save the materials used for the model to be used again.

Raw Materials

In designing your project, don't forget to consider available sections of wood you will be using. Remember that the actual size of the wood is fractionally smaller than the nominal size by which it is sold. Trueing up the wood will result in an even smaller dimension. You have to decide before you begin your design whether you will use standard sized sections or plane larger sections down to the exact sizes you will need. If your work will be done mainly with off-the-shelf sizes, you may find it helpful to keep remnants of the various cross sections so that you know exactly the size you can expect to buy. Don't forget though to mark out the work from the actual wood you are using for a job rather than relying on nominal sizes or even samples of wood from another job.

The same is true for sheet materials. Sheets are sold in standard sizes and parts thereof and if you take this into consideration, you can avoid wasting material or having to buy a whole sheet for an extra piece. You may be able to adjust the design slightly to take into account the available sizes of sheet materials.

Cutting lists

Once you have prepared your working drawings and decided on the dimensions of the material you are using you are ready to make up a detailed cutting list of all the components you will need. To start with, write down all the individual parts of the structure, either naming the parts clearly or numbering them.

Alongside each part, record the material from which it will be cut—softwood, hardwood or sheet material, and note the type and quality required. In the next column write down the cross section for rails or thickness for sheet material and note whether this dimension is nominal or actual. Sheet thicknesses are accurate enough to be treated as actual measurements although you will have to consider veneered or plastic coated materials which may be slightly thicker than standard.

Next, add the length of each rail or the dimensions length first and then width of each panel. On rails, make sure you have allowed enough for joints that will be cut at the ends and on boards remember to have the grain all running in the same direction. Finally add enough to each dimension to allow for cutting, planing and squaring of cut ends. Generally add $\frac{1}{2}$ in. (12mm) to the length of rails and $\frac{1}{4}$ in. (6mm) to each dimension for panels.

If you intend to order your materials as a "lot" which you will be cutting to size yourself, add up the total length you need of each cross sectional size of wood and add up the areas of panels of sheet materials. Then round the wood length up the nearest foot or half meter and the sheet areas to the number of whole sheets or standard parts thereof and place your order. If you are ordering small quantities of wood which you want to have cut individually by a retailer, reorganize your list so that quantities of similar items are grouped together.

A simple coffee table for example, would have its components listed as follows:

4 legs in teak, 1½ in. (38mm) square, 16 in. (406mm) long
4 rails in teak, 1 × 2 in. (25 × 50mm), 24 in. (610mm) long
1 top in teak veneered chipboard, ¾ in. (18mm) thick, 28 in. (710mm) square

The top will have to be cut from a 30 in. (760mm) board. You will therefore have to finish off the cut edges with matching iron-on teak edging or some form of molding.

Make a separate list of all the other things you need to put your design together including fixing devices such as nails and screws, hardware like hinges and catches and finishing materials like sandpaper, paints and varnishes. With everything you need listed out like this, you can be fairly sure that you will be able to get on with your work and not have to stop to go out to buy a forgotten component.

To show you how this works with a more complex piece such as the side table we have designed, here is the fully detailed cutting list, including allowances for cutting and planing. Note that each part on the cutting list is numbered; these numerals are also marked on the isometric drawing (page 127).

128

Ordering materials

Check suppliers in your area before you decide where to place your order. Ask neighbors where they get their materials and which yard they recommend for wood, hardware and so on. Call local firms to ask if they can handle large orders and if they will fill small orders and if they will cut materials to size. Ask if they will take an order over the telephone and get it ready for you to pick up or if you will have to wait for it there. If you need a particular brand of product, check that they stock it before you make the trip.

Once you have done this sort of investigation, shopping for supplies will become a lot easier. You will know where to buy the things you need and where to get the best prices and the best service. Keep a record of all this information as you acquire it in a notebook with A to Z listings and enter product names as well as suppliers and manufacturers. A notebook like this will be invaluable.

Tool check

The other important thing you should be doing at the same time as you are ordering materials is to give your tool kit a thorough check. The first point to note is whether you have all the tools you will need for the job you are planning. Think through the whole process from start to finish and write down all the tools you'll need at each stage. You will have to decide whether to buy tools you need for specialist jobs or see whether you can improvise using the tools you already have.

When you are sure you have the tools you will need check that they are in good condition. Pay particular attention to edge tools like saws, planes and chisels. If you will be doing woodwork regularly, get into the habit of sharpening and cleaning your tools as soon as you have finished work. If you don't do woodworking on a regular basis, check all the tools as you start each job so that the flow of work is not interrupted by having to sharpen and clean tools. Check too that you have enough replacement supplies for tools like drills, knives and frame saws.

Cutting list for side table

All parts cut from veneered chipboard $\frac{3}{4}$ in. (18mm) wide

Part	Cut	Plank width	Mark out to this size	Finished size
1: top	One	12 in. (305mm)	$21\frac{1}{4}$ in. (540mm) long	21 in. (533mm) long
2: shelf	Two	12 in. (305mm)	$20\frac{9}{16}$ in. (522mm) long	$20\frac{5}{16}$ in. (516mm) long
3: end	One	12 in. (305mm)	$17\frac{9}{16}$ in. (446mm) long	$17\frac{5}{16}$ in. (440mm) long
4: side	Two	6 in. (150mm)	$17\frac{9}{16}$ in. (446mm) long	$17\frac{5}{16}$ in. (440mm) long
5: divider	Two	12 in. (150mm)	$10\frac{7}{8} \times 8\frac{1}{4}$ in. (276 × 210mm)	$10\frac{5}{8} \times 8$ in. (270 × 200mm)

CHAPTER 9
Assembly

Armed with accurate working drawings, all the raw materials and tools in good working order, you are probably anxious to get started on the actual construction of what you have designed. But before you do, you must learn the ten commandments of woodwork construction, a sequence of operations that can be applied to any project large or small, to ensure that everything gets done in the right order and nothing is forgotten. If you follow these rules you should have no problems.

1. Set out all the parts if they have been ordered cut roughly to size. If not, cut everything to size first and number adjacent pieces.
2. Mark pieces to exact length using a marking knife and a square for accuracy and then cut them to size.
3. Mark out the joints, cross checking with your drawings that each is of the right type and is in the right place.
4. Double check everything.
5. Cut the joints after hatching in all waste areas with pencil to avoid mistakes.
6. Fit the joints together to test them, tapping gently with a mallet or hammer and a block of scrap wood so that you don't damage the wood. Don't force a tight joint.
7. Dismantle the joints, ease tight spots and clean up with a smoothing plane and sandpaper any surfaces that will be inaccessible when

the structure is glued up and assembled.
8. Glue up and assemble the joints, clamping if necessary. Check that the structure is held squarely and is not twisted by the clamps and that all joints are closed up tight. This is your last chance to make any corrections or adjustments. Wipe off any excess glue.
9. When the glue has set, remove the clamps and clean up the outside surfaces of the structure with a smoothing plane and sandpaper, removing any pencil or knife marks. Round all sharp corners slightly with sandpaper unless it is a feature of the design to keep them totally square.
10. Apply the surface finish before attaching any of the fittings and other hardware.

Applying these rules to the construction of the side table designed in the last chapter will show how they work in reality.

A look at the cutting list is the starting point. This is a simple project because all the parts are cut from the same type of board, veneered chipboard, and the board is readily available in the two widths necessary which will save having to apply veneer edging to cut edges afterwards. The cutting list tells us that there are six components cut from 12 in. (305mm) board—the top, center shelf, bottom, end and two dividers—and two components cut

from 6 in. (150mm) wide board— the two narrow side pieces.

Mark out these pieces on the boards with an added $\frac{1}{4}$ in. (6mm) allowance for squaring up included in the measurements. Square each cutting line around the board with a try square and marking knife so that when the cuts are made the line will be clean and the veneer will not split or tear. Note that the allowance for squaring up is added to each measurement so that there is a gap of $\frac{1}{2}$ in. (12mm) between adjacent pieces on the board. Until you are really good at sawing accurately leaving this sort of margin is a good safety measure in case you cut inaccurately or the saw jumps out of the cut. Then number each piece.

Now you can cut the planks into their component parts, sawing carefully on the waste side of each line and supporting the overhanging part of the board as you near the end of each cut so that it doesn't break off and split the workpiece.

With all the components cut out, the next step is to clean up the cut ends using a smoothing plane and shooting board so you don't split the edge veneer. Be careful not to plane below the knife line marking the extent of the workpiece.

Next mark out the joints. These are butt joints in every case except where the two narrow side pieces join the center shelf. Here we are using full lap joints which means a cut-out has to be made in the edges of the shelf and base pieces. The length of each cut-out will be the same as the width of the side pieces that fit into them, so lay one of the side pieces over first the shelf and then the base, aligning their edges accurately, and use the marking knife to make two short lines near the edge of shelf and base.

The width of the cut-outs will be exactly the thickness of the board being used, so the next job is to set the marking gauge to exactly the thickness of the board and use it to mark the other edge of the cut-out. A quick check with the end of a side piece on each component will show that no mistakes have been made and that the cut-out exactly matches the width and thickness of the piece that will fit into it. Hatch in the waste area with pencil and saw the cut-out using a panel saw for the longer cut and tenon saw for the shorter one. Be extremely careful not to overshoot the cutting marks by bringing the saw blade up to the vertical as you approach the end of each cut.

Although the other joints in the unit are butt joints, they will need some reinforcement in a material that is as brittle as chipboard is along the edges. Using dowel pegs is a good idea since they are invisible once the joint is completed and add considerable strength to each joint. Dowels $\frac{3}{8}$ in. (9mm) in diameter will suit the board thickness well.

Three dowels will be sufficient for the 12 in. (305mm) wide joints, two for the 6 in. (150mm) wide ones. The next step is to mark center lines along all meeting edges

and then mark the dowel positions on paired edges in turn. The dowel spacing is about 3 in. (75mm) in each case.

You will need to use a depth stop to drill the dowel holes, especially those at right angles to the board's length. These should be $\frac{1}{2}$ in. (12mm) deep and those parallel to the board's length should be between 1 and $1\frac{1}{2}$ in. (25 and 38mm) deep. Drill them carefully, making sure that the holes are vertical and cut the dowels to a fraction less than the depth of the combined hole depth. Cut grooves in the dowel pegs to allow excess glue to escape. Note that the dowels joining the dividers to the center shelf pass right through the shelf.

With all the holes drilled and the dowels cut, test assemble the joints to check fit. Test for lack of squareness at the dowel joints and re-drill new holes if necessary $\frac{1}{2}$ in. (12mm) away from those that don't meet correctly.

When you are satisfied that everything fits exactly as it should, you can prepare for the actual assembly. Start at the bottom, joining the wide end piece and the two narrower side pieces to the base by gluing the dowels and the joining edges and pressing each joint together tightly. Then add the lower divider, the center shelf and the upper divider, checking the alignment of each piece in turn. Finally add the top.

131

A unit of this shape is difficult to clamp up in the usual way. The likely trouble spots are around the small bookshelf and here a long or sash clamp holding the narrow sides together, plus some weight on the top over the dividers should ensure that the joints stay tight. Check the open end and side for squareness before leaving the glue to set, and tap any joints that are not completely closed with a mallet or hammer before the glue has hardened too much.

When the glue has set, remove the clamps and weights and sand down all the outside surfaces of the unit ready for finishing. Fix the castors after it is finished.

The second stage is to add the lower divider, the center shelf and the upper divider, checking each piece for alignment

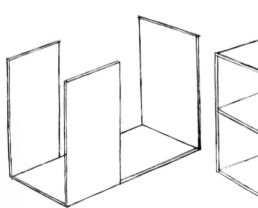

The first stage in assembling the chair side table is to join the end and side pieces to the base

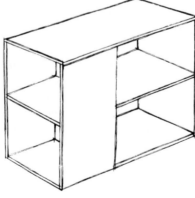

The third and final stage is to add the top. Before clamping the assembly, check that all the joints are tight and square

Some additional points about assembly

The assembly of the side table has illustrated many of the points involved in making things of wood, but there are some that because of its design it did not cover. Here are some of these points.

On a structure with a number of identical components, such as a series of side rails of the same length and with the same joints at each end, always mark up all the components together, squaring lines across all edges at the same time and cutting matching pairs to length clamped together. This minimizes the chance of a cumulative error occurring in the measurements and it also speeds up the process.

On constructions that involve making up frameworks, try to divide the work up into sections that can be assembled and clamped individually first. A dining chair is a good example. Here, each side of the chair—front and back legs, seat and bottom rails—would be assembled, clamped up and left to dry. Then the two frames can be linked by the front and back seat rails and the foot rails, and clamped again and allowed to set without the risk of the clamping disturbing the joints in the two side frames. You can use this technique for many constructions of this sort.

There are two vital points to remember when you are using clamps. The first is always to insert protective packing pieces of wood or cardboard between the jaws of the clamp and the workpiece to protect the surface from damage when the clamps are tightened. The second is not to over-tighten the clamps, since you are likely to either damage the work or pull it out of square if you do. Always check that what you have clamped is square by measuring across the diagonals with a steel tape or more accurately with a device called a squaring rod which you can easily make up from a thin hardwood batten with an angled end. To check a diagonal with the rod, push the angled end into one corner of the structure and lay the other end of the rod over the opposite corner. Make a pencil mark on the rod at the overlap point and then reverse the rod to measure the other diagonal. The mark should lie exactly over the second corner indicating that the diagonals are the same and that the structure is square.

When joints are to be reinforced with nails or screws, don't drive them through the joint until the glue has set and the clamps have been removed. The joint doesn't need reinforcing until it is in use and trying to drive nails or screws into joints that are freshly glued can have the effect of forcing them out of square.

When you have left wooden horns protruding at corners—on haunched tenons, for example—saw off the excess wood when the clamps have been removed. Don't try to cut too close with the saw though. It is better to saw off all but approximately $\frac{1}{16}$ in. (1.5mm) to avoid any risk of the saw teeth marking the side of the work against which you are cutting, and then to plane off the remainder for a perfectly smooth and flush finish. Use a shooting board to avoid splitting end grain.

Useful geometry

Marking wood out is easy if everything is in squares and rectangles. But if what you have designed includes circles, ovals and other curves, not to mention angles other than 90°, then you will need a little geometry to help you to mark out the pieces accurately. A set of compasses makes circles easy to draw, but will not cope with large circumferences. For these, you can make up a simple device from a piece of softwood with a nail driven into one end to act as a compass point and a hole drilled in the other end to take a pencil. The distance between nail and pencil hole is set to the radius of the circle you want to draw, and the nail is held over the center while the wood is rotated so that the pencil will mark out the circle.

Improvised compasses—a length of softwood or a piece of string

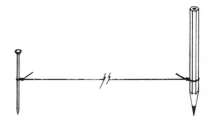

Ellipses are more difficult. To draw one, start with a line AB as long as you want the ellipse to be. At the mid-point of AB draw a line CD at right angles to AB and as long as the width of the ellipse. Set two tacks along AB so that the distance of each from D is equal to half the length of the ellipse (AB). Tie a loop of string around the tacks so that it just reaches D when held taut with a pencil. Keeping the string taut, move the pencil around in a curve and it will trace out a perfect ellipse on the surface. To draw other complex curves, you can buy curved templates from art supply stores.

Making angles which are 30°, 60° and even 45° if you don't have a combination square is quite straightforward. You can construct the angles with your compass. To draw a 60° angle, first draw a semicircle on A as center. Then place the point of the compass at B, keeping the radius the same and draw an arc at C and join C to A to give you the desired angle of 60°. Then to bisect this into 30°, place the point of the compass on B and draw an arc. Repeat this on C, making the arc you draw intersect with the one drawn on B and then join up A to the intersection at D to create a 30° angle. Also follow this procedure to bisect a right angle to make a 45° angle.

The last geometry trick you may find useful involves dividing a surface up into strips of equal width. This can involve some very tricky mental arithmetic on awkward widths, but the solution is quite simple. Suppose you want to divide a board 4½ in. (114mm) wide into five equal parts. Take a ruler and hold it at an angle across the board near one end with the zero over one edge of the board and the 5 in. (125mm) mark over the other edge. Make a mark on the board at each intermediate mark on the ruler and repeat the process at the other end of the board. Join the marks with a straight edge to create the five equal strips.

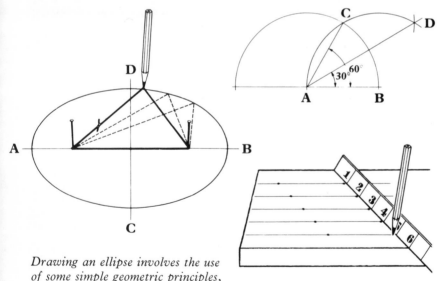

Constructing angles of 60 and 30°; all you need is a pair of compasses and a ruler

Drawing an ellipse involves the use of some simple geometric principles, two pins, a piece of string and a pencil

Dividing a surface up into several strips of equal width, using a ruler and pencil

Avoiding mistakes and correcting them

There is only one way to avoid mistakes in woodworking and that is to be careful at every stage of the process from first drawing to last cut. Double check every measurement, particularly when you transfer dimensions from drawings to wood and when you are marking out joints and don't do anything irreversible like starting to cut or chisel or drill until you are confident that you are doing it in the right place. But no one is perfect and mistakes do happen however careful you are.

Probably the easiest mistake to make is to cut a piece too short. You may be able to use it elsewhere in the construction by cutting it to a smaller correct size, but if you cannot, it will have to be replaced and saved for another project.

Cutting a joint too loose is an equally common error but here there are remedies for the situation. You may be able to insert a sliver of wood into the joint to fill the gap or to drive wedges in above or below the joint to tighten it up. This is particularly effective for joints like the mortise and tenon, if the mortise was cut overlong. Wedges driven in above and below the tenon will not only make the joint tight if they are glued before being driven in, but they will fill the gaps left thereby enabling the mistake to be almost completely disguised with a little careful finishing.

If you find when you assemble a framework that the construction is slightly out of square, you may be able to make some slight adjustments to one or more of the corner joints, by paring away the shoulder of a tenon or the bottom of a housing, for example. Using shrinkage plates allows you to make slight adjustments in fixing table tops and panels that are slightly out of alignment.

As a last resort, you may have no alternative but to dismantle something that you cannot remedy. With a glued up assembly you can't afford to take too long to make this decision as modern woodworking glues set quite quickly. Once the glue sets, you may do more damage by trying to take the pieces apart. When you do dismantle something, try to clean off as much glue as you can before doing any remedial work. The components will have to be re-glued and fixed in their original positions and they won't join well if there is already a layer of glue on the wood. Try to find the fault, re-cutting any components that prove to be undersized or not square and test assemble the pieces. This can be a lot of extra work, but it is better to correct faults than to live with furniture that will always remind you of your mistakes.

Using wood scraps

Never throw away a piece of wood that could be useful. Wood isn't cheap nowadays and every scrap of a reasonable size can be used sometime, somewhere. There are always small-scale projects, like wooden toys for children that can be made using scraps. And there are always times when you need a small piece of wood to support a shelf or act as a batten. If you keep a box of scraps you can always rely on having a piece on hand that is the right size and shape for the job.

Obviously the amount of wood you save has to be sensible. You can't keep every end you saw off. Keep scraps of around 4 in. (100mm) in length for softwood and about 6 in. (150mm) square for sheet materials. Keep pieces of this size in a box or basket under the workbench or in a corner of your workshop. This then serves as a sort of waste basket for wood scraps so that the floor doesn't become littered with them.

Larger pieces that qualify as stock should be stored in the main store of wood and sheet materials in racks or shelves. They could turn out to be a valuable collection that will save you those annoying trips to the store for a few feet of wood or a piece of sheet material.

CHAPTER 10
A fine finish

Sanding the surface

Once the assembly of the piece you are making is completed, you have to prepare the surface ready for whatever finish you are going to apply. The first stage is to use an abrasive paper to smooth down the wood surface.

Abrasive papers have a variety of mineral coatings stuck to a paper backing. Glass is the most common, but granules of garnet, emery and silicon carbide are also used. Abrasive paper is commonly called sandpaper even though sand is no longer used for this purpose.

Glasspaper and garnet paper are used for smoothing bare wood and silicon carbide paper is used for sanding down paintwork on both wood and metal. It can be used wet or dry. Emery paper is used only on metal.

All these papers come in a variety of grades, from very coarse to fine. Whichever you are using, the principle is always the same. Start with a coarse paper or a medium-grade one if the wood surface is already fairly smooth and finish up with the finest grade. Remember that a coarse paper, no matter how worn smooth it is, will never give a fine finish.

Always use an abrasive paper with a sanding block so that you can sand evenly all over the surface. If you use your hand you will invariably press harder on some points than others. Sand *along* the grain, never across it; if you do you will mark the wood and these marks are very difficult to remove.

Abrasive paper will not work well if either it or the wood is damp, so always keep it in a dry place. If it gets clogged by use on resinous wood, you can clear its cutting edges by pulling the back of the sheet over the edge of your work bench. This also makes the sheet more flexible.

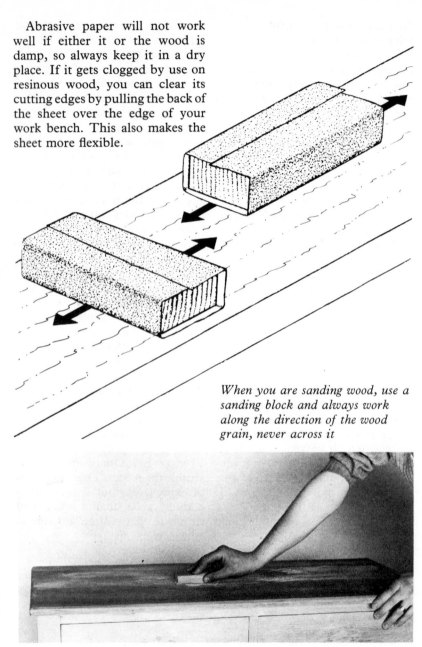

When you are sanding wood, use a sanding block and always work along the direction of the wood grain, never across it

136

Stopping and filling

When you have sanded the surface smooth, wipe it over with a fine brush to remove the dust, brushing along the grain. If there are any defects in the surface like pinholes, splits or small knots, you can fill them with matching plastic wood or a wood stopper. These are available in many wood shades or you can make them any color you like by adding a few drops of the appropriate wood stain. Press the wood stopper into the hole and let it dry slightly proud of the surface. Then you can sand it flush afterwards for an invisible repair.

If you are intending to paint the wood, you can smooth a grainy surface by filling it with a very fine surface filler, which is mixed to a fairly fluid consistency and then rubbed over the wood surface. When it has dried it can then be sanded absolutely smooth ready for the paint to be applied. Professional woodworkers use wood fillers to smooth the grain of certain woods which are then sanded and finished with a natural finish.

Fill defects such as pinholes, knots and splits by using a matching wood stopper or plastic wood. Fill the hole slightly proud of the surface, and sand it down flush when it has dried

The finishes you can use

You will have decided at the design stage what finish your piece will have. Whatever type you are using, there are a couple of points to remember. First, dust will ruin almost every finish, so try to work in a still, dust-free atmosphere. Most finishes are best applied at room temperature. Excess heat or cold may affect drying time and final appearance, as will damp. If you're finishing small pieces, work on a sheet of hardboard or heavy cardboard to avoid staining your bench. With large pieces, raise them off the floor on blocks or place them across two sawhorses or trestles.

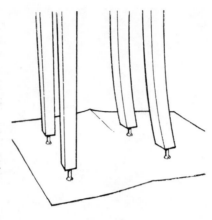

Above: smaller pieces, especially chairs and small tables, can be raised off the floor so that the legs can be painted by the simple trick of driving screws or tapping nails into the bottom of the legs. Remove them when the finish is dry

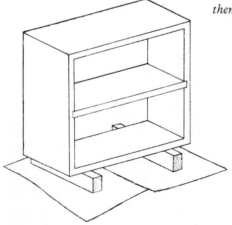

When you are painting or varnishing large pieces of furniture, raise them off the floor on blocks so you can paint right down to the bottom of each side

Natural finishes

Natural finishes are those finishes that enhance the color and grain pattern of the wood but leave it clearly visible. The cheapest and simplest is linseed oil, which is available in both raw and boiled forms. Boiled linseed oil dries more quickly and is easier to apply if mixed first with equal parts of turpentine. To put it on, simply pour it onto the wood and rub it in well with a lintfree cloth. Leave it for an hour or two, then wipe off the excess oil. Leave it to dry for a couple of days before applying a second coat. On woods that are naturally oily, such as teak, two coats will suffice, but others may need up to four coats. Softwoods are unsuitable for oiled finishes, however, as they become dirty and discolored very quickly.

Teak oil contains drying agents which speed up the drying process and resists marking of the surface more readily than linseed oil. Olive oil is preferable for oiling wooden articles which may come into contact with food—bowls and chopping boards, for example.

Wax polishes can be applied to most woods, but are not very durable and need frequent renewing to keep them in good condition. They are more effective as a protective finish when used over another finish such as varnish. Apply a heavy coat, work it well into the wood surface and leave to dry for several hours before rubbing with a soft brush or cloth.

Varnish is the most durable of

the natural finishes and is easy to apply and to maintain. There are several finishes available, ranging from matt through semi-gloss to full gloss. You apply them directly to the sanded wood, rubbing the first coat, thinned down with turpentine, into the surface along the grain with a cloth and putting on four or five subsequent coats with a brush for a really superb finish. Sand down lightly with fine glasspaper between coats.

French polish is a traditional natural finish applied to much antique furniture. It is rarely used by the home craftsman except to restore antique furniture. To make jobs like this easier, there are various brands of French polish available and it is best to use these unless you are experienced in the skills of French polishing.

Transparent color finishes
This group of finishes includes wood stains and colored sealers, both of which alter the color of the wood, often quite dramatically, while leaving the grain pattern still visible. Both are best used on light colored woods.

Stains come in two types. The first is a solvent-based variety, the second a water-based one. Stains of one type can be intermixed with other colors of the same type to produce intermediate shades, or can be thinned with the appropriate thinner to produce weaker colors.

The bare wood surface must be clean and free of any existing finish, particularly wax or oil. Apply the stain either with a cloth or a brush, applying it evenly to avoid overlaps and working along the grain. Then let the stain dry thoroughly. Be sure to have good ventilation in the workroom if you're using a solvent-based type. If you want to apply a second coat to get a deeper color, sand the surface lightly first and wipe it clean and then apply the second coat again working evenly and avoiding overlapping the strokes.

Stained wood has no surface protection, so it is usual to finish it with a clear varnish, applied in the same way as on unstained wood.

A quicker way of getting a stain finish is to use a colored sealer, which is a stain and a varnish combined. It is applied just like a transparent varnish. However, the depth of color you achieve is less with colored sealers as the stain cannot soak into the wood when it is mixed into varnish.

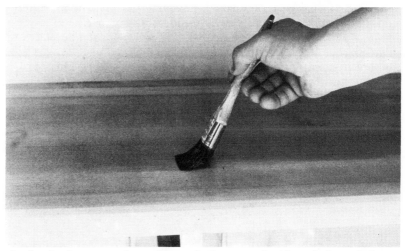

Apply the first coat of varnish to the bare wood with a cloth, and then add further coats with a brush, sanding between coats

Opaque finishes

If you want a hard-wearing finish to your work and don't mind covering the wood surface, then paint is the finish to choose. There's a wide selection of colors in different sorts of finish. Traditionally, oil-based paints were always used on wood, but paint manufacturers have now formulated water-based products that are equally hard-wearing, easier to apply and quicker to dry and odorless.

To get a good finish on wood with paint, you have to build up several coats. The first coat you apply is a primer, which helps to fill the grain structure and provides good adhesion for subsequent coats. Next comes the undercoat, a highly pigmented paint that conceals the color of the primer. Last of all come the top coats of the paint finish you choose—usually semi-gloss or gloss. Two coats give the best and most hard-wearing finish to your work. For a really fine finish, don't put too much paint on with each coat and sand down lightly between coats.

Hardware

Apart from hinges, already discussed in Chapter 7, there are a number of other various items of hardware which you may need to complete a project.

Catches hold small doors and flaps closed. There are many different types. One of the most useful and simple to fit is the magnetic catch, which comes in a variety of shapes and sizes. The magnet is housed in a plastic casing which is usually attached to the piece of furniture and a small metal plate is fixed to the door or flap. The plate is attracted by the magnet as it approaches it and so holds the door or flap shut.

The ball catch has a spring-loaded ball bearing mounted in a housing which is usually screwed to the door or flap to be held shut. The ball springs into a recess or a hole in a striking plate fixed to the inside of the door recess.

Mechanical catches have a spring-mounted peg or roller fixed to the door or flap. This springs into position over a stop plate when the door is closed and springs back when it is opened.

Automatic catches have a latch mechanism housed in a metal casing mounted in the cupboard, and a latch hook attached to the door or flap. The hook engages in the latch mechanism when the door or flap is closed, but is released simply by applying pressure to the door. So it's ideal for use where handles would look obtrusive and can be opened with elbow pressure even when your hands are full.

To hold doors and the like more permanently shut, you need a bolt or even a lock. The simplest barrel bolt consists of two parts, the bolt and its catch plate, both of which are screwed to the work. For a neater and less obtrusive finish you can buy recessed bolts which are set into the face of the door or furniture.

The simplest lock is also a surface-fixing device. You screw the lock mechanism to the back of the door, flush with the closing edge, and the striking plate is screwed to the furniture to match up with the lock position. All you have to do to complete the fixing is to drill a keyhole through the door and cover it if you wish with a small escutcheon plate.

The barrel lock is a flush-fitting lock inserted in a hole drilled in the door or drawer. Turning the key rotates a hooked retainer through 90° to engage on a striker plate on the inside.

The mortise lock is the strongest and neatest type of lock to fit. As its name implies, it is housed in a mortise cut in the edge of the door, and so needs careful and accurate fitting. The striking plate is recessed into the door surround.

Flaps, although fitted with hinges and catches, often need another piece of hardware to keep them in a horizontal position. The simplest flap stay is a length of chain attached to both the flap and the furniture. This pulls taut and supports the flap when it is fully open. A stronger device is the folding stay, a two-part stay that folds out straight when the flap is open. This type can be used on lift-up flaps as well. The sliding stay has a rigid arm screwed to the flap. Its other end either slides through a fixed mounting or along a special channel. The friction stay is similar in principle, but the mechanism incorporates a friction device that controls the speed at which the flap opens—a useful feature on heavy drop flaps.

Knobs and handles come in an enormous range of types and sizes, from the simple screw-in knob to the continuous strip type found on much modern furniture. There is a choice with many handles of face fixing with wood screws driven through countersunk holes in the handle, or concealed fixing with small bolts passing through the surface from behind. The continuous strip type is usually housed in a groove cut in the door.

Shelves can be supported on simple blocks, on small shelf supports set into the sides of the shelving unit or hooking onto bookcase strip, on brackets of various types or by means of adjustable shelf support systems.

Drawers rarely need special equipment, but there are times when you may want to be able to pull a drawer all the way out to expose its contents. For this you need the special type of drawer runner fitted to filing cabinets and the like, and consisting of two steel tracks which interlock and hold the drawer firmly when it is opened.

Finally, sliding doors need at least some sort of track to slide in, and may also need suspending by their top edges if they are too heavy to slide otherwise. There is a wide range of sliding door devices available for every purpose from small closet doors up to garage doors.

Brass-plated knobs and pulls are available in a vast array of designs, traditional and modern

Stencils and transfers

Once you have applied the finish to your workpiece, and added such hardware as is needed, you may want to add further decoration to it. One way of doing this is to paint on designs using a stencil, a paper, cardboard or plastic mask through which you can either brush or spray on paint. You can either cut out your own stencils, or buy ready-cut ones from arts and crafts suppliers. Be careful when you use them that the paint doesn't creep under the edges of the stencil and mark the surrounding areas. One way of doing this is to stick the stencil down with peelable rubber adhesive—the type used for scrapbooks. This won't damage the finish already on the wood, and allows you to peel the stencil away after you've painted through it.

If it's simple squares, lines and geometric shapes you want, you can use masking tape instead to outline the area you want to paint and guarantee perfectly straight edges. Press the tape down firmly to stop the paint from creeping under the edges.

An alternative way of applying decorative touches is to use decals or transfers, which you can now buy in an enormous range of designs. Some are the traditional paper-backed type, which you soak in water before sliding the decal off and into position on the surface you're decorating. Others are self-adhesive; you simply peel away the backing paper and press them down. This type is more difficult to

Decorative decals bring a touch of color to painted surfaces

remove if you decide to change the design but is also more durable. With either type, be careful not to trap air bubbles underneath as you press them into place. You can avoid this by starting in the center and pressing with a circular motion out towards the edges.

Simple renovation

Perhaps the simplest renovation job is to strip the old finish off a piece of furniture and then refinish it just to improve its looks. As you probably won't know what the old finish is, you will have to try a number of solvents in turn. Begin with turpentine, which will remove wax polishes. If that doesn't work, move on to denatured alcohol (methylated spirits), which will soften French polish after about five minutes, allowing you to scrape the finish off. The next solvent to try is cellulose thinner, which will budge cellulose-based finishes and also oil varnish. If you still haven't removed the finish, your last resort will be a chemical paint stripper, which will strip off modern paints and varnishes that other solvents don't affect and which is also good at removing old paints and varnish stains too.

Whichever solvent you have to use, make sure you do a thorough removal job, rubbing the wood surface with fine steel wool as you work the solvent in to make sure that you remove all the finish. When you get down to bare wood, you may find that there are a number of small blemishes that need repairing either by filling or sanding before you apply a new finish.

Stripping old finishes using the appropriate solvent can be a messy and time-consuming job . . .

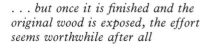

. . . but once it is finished and the original wood is exposed, the effort seems worthwhile after all

143

Veneer repairs

If there are patches of veneer that are split and lifting, slit the veneer with a sharp razor blade, following the grain line carefully. Then use a strip of thin springy metal, such as an oil-painter's palette knife to apply a small amount of wood-working glue under both sides of the split. Finally, weight down or clamp the repair for a few hours, with a piece of paper between the wood and the weight so that any glue oozing out will stick to the paper and can be sponged off later.

Larger areas of damage will have to be patched with fresh veneer. Lay the new veneer over the damaged area, and use a sharp knife to cut through both layers. Then prize up the damaged piece and scrape away the old glue before gluing the new patch in place and weighting it down as before.

Many handicraft suppliers sell sheets of veneer in a wide range of wood types, and you should be able to find one with a grain pattern and color that is a reasonable match for the rest of the piece. If you cannot, you may have to experiment with wood stains on a paler veneer to achieve exactly the color you want. As a last resort you may have to strip some veneer from a less noticeable area of the piece to make the repair.

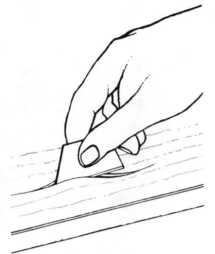

Splits or areas of veneer that have lifted should be opened up carefully with a razor blade

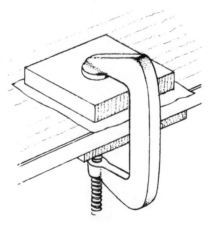

After working glue under the veneer, the repair should be clamped for several hours to allow the glue to set

Dents and scores

Dents and scores often lend character to an old piece of furniture, but they can be repaired reasonably well if they are unsightly. To smooth out a dent, first carefully remove any finish from the dented area. Then apply a hot electric iron to the dent over several layers of damp cloth, like pressing a shirt. The steam is forced into the wood fibers and causes the wood to swell and fill out the dent. You may have to apply heat several times to raise a dent completely. Softwoods respond to this treatment more readily than do hardwoods.

Scores that have merely scratched the finish can be touched up simply by repairing the finish at the point of damage. Deeper scratches should be cleaned and then touched in with the same finish as the rest of the surface, using an artists' paint brush, to disguise the end grain exposed by the scratch. Then the area around the scratch can be refinished to match.

Deep holes or gashes should be filled with a wood stopper in a color that matches that of the surrounding wood. Score the surface of the filler with a needle to match the surrounding grain pattern when it is nearly dry, and then refinish to match the surrounding area.

You can lift out dents by using a damp cloth and a hot iron

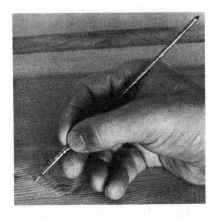

Disguise deep scratches by touching in the edges of the cut using an artist's brush

Stains and burns

Spots and rings made by hot plates and wet glasses can be difficult to remove from less durable finishes. Some people swear by a paste of water and cigarette ash, others by a mixture of raw linseed oil and turpentine applied with a rag. If these don't work, try rubbing the stain with fine steel wool moistened with linseed oil. If the stain has penetrated right through the finish, all you can do is strip the finish back to bare wood, and refinish the area to match its surroundings. If the surface is repeatedly stained in this way, strip it completely, and then use a wood bleach to remove the stain.

Burns are almost always caused by cigarettes. If it's merely a scorch, you may be able to remove it in the same way as a stain. A deeper burn will have to be scraped clean with a knife. This will leave a dent which you can then raise with the hot iron treatment already described. On veneers, you will have to cut out and patch the damaged area since it is likely that the burn will have penetrated right through the veneer into the board surface beneath. Clean out all the burned wood and fill the hole with wood filler to the level of the board surface before repairing the veneer surface.

Splits and damaged joints

Splits in frames and panels can often simply be glued and clamped back together again. If a part has actually split off, try to glue it back again if you have the piece, otherwise you will have to cut out a regular-shaped plug of wood and use this to make a patch, cutting out a recess in the furniture into which the plug is glued. When the glue has set, the patch can then be shaped to match the surrounding surface.

The simplest way of repairing damaged joints, such as those in a chair frame, is to saw through the tenons or tongues of the joint and use dowels to remake the joint. Dowels can also be used to reinforce splits and other damage at hinges.

Refinishing

Once you have removed all the old finish and carried out any necessary repairs, all that's left is to refinish the piece, using one of the finishes already discussed. As long as you have removed *all* the old finish and done the repairs carefully, the results you get should give you a piece of furniture that is, almost literally, like new. And you will have the satisfaction of knowing that the restoration is all your own work.

CHAPTER 11
Projects—making things for your workshop

A bench hook

One of the first things you can make for your workshop is a bench hook. You'll remember from Chapter 5 that this invaluable bench aid is used to hold small sections of wood steady while they are sawn on the bench top. It's not a saw guide, so it does not have to be made extremely accurately. That's why it is a good first project, for you to get the feel of your tools.

All you need to make it is a piece of wood for the base, and two smaller pieces to form the blocks that are fixed at each end of the base. The base should be at least $\frac{3}{4}$ in. (18mm) thick, and should if possible be of a hardwood such as beech or oak. You can use softwood, which will be cheaper and easier to find, but the bench hook you make with it will not last as long. A piece of blockboard or thick plywood would do instead.

The base should measure about 8 in. (200mm) in length and 6 in. (150mm) in width. If you have to buy a piece of wood, it will already be sawn or planed to about the width you want. Buy a foot (305mm), and you will be able to mark and cut the ends squarely, finishing up with the length that you want. Mark one end square with your try square, and cut it to length carefully with the handsaw. Then sand down the cut end, rounding off the corners slightly. Next, measure 8 in. (200mm) along the wood, and mark the other end square at this point. Cut here too, and sand down the end.

The two end blocks are each cut from wood measuring about $1 \times 1\frac{1}{2}$ in. (25 × 38mm), and each is about 5 in. (125mm) long, so you should be able to cut both from a one foot length of the right-sized wood. Square and cut one end first, then mark out and cut the first block. If this cut is made square, you can measure out and mark the end of the second block from this cut. Sand each cut end.

Because the bench hook will be used to saw on, it is best that no metal fixings are used to attach the blocks to the base. The saw could slip and blunt its teeth on a screw or nail head. Instead attach them with dowels. Lay one block in place over the end of the base, with the gap on your right if you saw righthanded, on the left otherwise. Clamp it in position, and drill two holes down through the block and the base big enough to take dowels

$\frac{3}{8}$ in. (9mm) in diameter. Repeat this with the other block, to be fitted to the reverse side of the board, again drilling two dowel holes.

Now cut four dowels, each about 2 in. (50mm) long, glue the matching surface between block and base and tap the glued dowels into their holes. Make sure the blocks are pressed hard against the base by clamping them again, and leave to set. Then saw off the stub ends of the dowels, and plane the top surface of each block smooth. This will also level the ends of the dowels for a neat finish.

Cutting list for bench hook
Base: $8 \times 6 \times \frac{3}{4}$ in. (200 × 150 × 18mm)
Blocks: $5 \times 1\frac{1}{2} \times 1$ in. (125 × 38 × 25mm)
Dowels: 2 in. (50mm) long, $\frac{3}{8}$ in. (9mm) in diameter

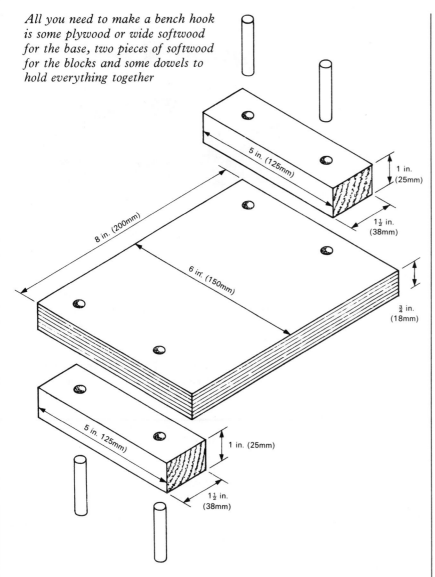

All you need to make a bench hook is some plywood or wide softwood for the base, two pieces of softwood for the blocks and some dowels to hold everything together

5 in. (125mm)

1 in. (25mm)

1½ in. (38mm)

8 in. (200mm)

6 in. (150mm)

¾ in. (18mm)

5 in. 125mm

1 in. (25mm)

1½ in. (38mm)

Miter block

The miter block is very similar in principle to the bench hook. It is used on the bench top in the same way, only this time the upper block is a saw guide as well as a surface against which the wood you're sawing is supported. The guides are at 45° to the workpiece, and allow you to cut mitered ends on small sections of wood. For larger pieces, it's better to use a miter box, which will be more accurate. Buy a ready-made one unless you are confident you can mark out and make the cuts that form the saw guides with the necessary accuracy.

For the miter block you will again need a base about ¾ in. (18mm) thick. The same material that you used for your bench hook will do admirably. The base once again should be about 6 in. (150mm) wide, but should be a little longer—about 10 in. (250mm). Mark it out and cut it to length as before.

The upper mitered guide should be of 1½ × 2 in. (38 × 50mm) wood, thick enough to guide the saw blade firmly during the cut. It is 10 in. (250mm) long, and is attached to the base along one long edge. As before, it is best to fix it in place with dowels, spaced as shown. Attach it first, and then mark the angled cuts to be made in it by using a combination square or using geometry. Make the cuts with the tenon saw, following the guide lines which you have drawn carefully on the wood.

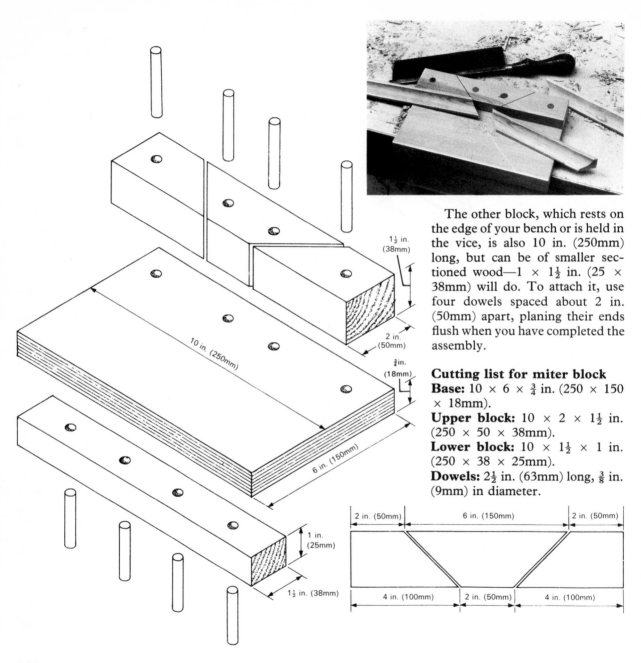

The other block, which rests on the edge of your bench or is held in the vice, is also 10 in. (250mm) long, but can be of smaller sectioned wood—1 × 1½ in. (25 × 38mm) will do. To attach it, use four dowels spaced about 2 in. (50mm) apart, planing their ends flush when you have completed the assembly.

Cutting list for miter block
Base: 10 × 6 × ¾ in. (250 × 150 × 18mm).
Upper block: 10 × 2 × 1½ in. (250 × 50 × 38mm).
Lower block: 10 × 1½ × 1 in. (250 × 38 × 25mm).
Dowels: 2½ in. (63mm) long, ⅜ in. (9mm) in diameter.

Oilstone box

You will buy your oilstone in a cardboard box, but this will not last very long around the workshop and will soon become very oily. It is also not very good for holding the stone while you are sharpening your plane or chisel blades. A custom-made wooden box is better all around.

The easiest way of making this is to make up a solid box—top, bottom and four sides—and then to saw it in half. This ensures that the two halves match exactly. To make it you will need two small pieces of $\frac{1}{2}$ in. (12mm) thick plywood to form the top and bottom of the box, some $\frac{1}{2} \times 1$ in. (12 × 25mm) softwood for the sides, and two small blocks of hardwood which are set at each end of the oilstone to allow you to use the whole area of the stone for sharpening—the blades can run off at each end without cutting into the softwood of the box.

Start by cutting the two small blocks of hardwood so that they match exactly the cross-section of the oilstone, and make sure you cut them with the end grain as shown overleaf. Place one at each end of the stone, and measure the length overall of the block-stone-block sandwich. Cut two pieces of the softwood to exactly this measurement and lay them alongside the stone. Now measure the width of the softwood-stone-softwood sandwich and cut two more pieces of softwood to form the ends of the oilstone box. Glue and nail the four sides of the box together after marking all around it the halfway line along which you will later saw the box in half. Do not drive nails near this line.

Now measure the dimensions of the box and cut two pieces of plywood slightly oversize to form the top and bottom of the box. Glue and nail each one in place using short nails so their points will not reach the halfway saw line, and plane the edges flush with the sides.

Next comes the tricky part—sawing the box in half along the marked line. Hold the box in your vise, long side uppermost and saw along the line through that side and to a point halfway down each end. Then turn the box over and complete the cut from the other side, being careful to make the two saw cuts meet exactly. Sand the cut

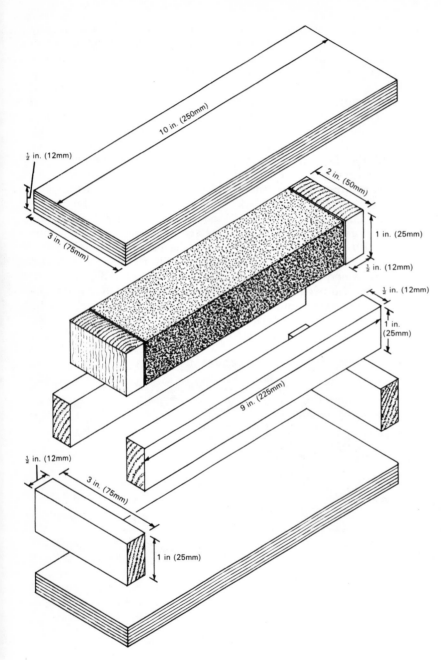

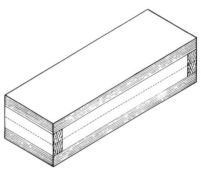

Left: an exploded view of the oilstone box. Above: a section through the box, with the stone sandwiched between the hardwood blocks, and the completed box

edges smooth, and insert the oilstone and wedge blocks in one half of the box, trimming the blocks if necessary to get a tight fit. Then put on the lid.

Cutting list for box for 8 × 2 × 1 in. (200 × 50 × 25mm) oilstone

Top/bottom: ½ in. (12mm) plywood 3 × 10 in. (75 × 250mm).
Sides: ½ × 1 in. (12 × 25mm) softwood, 9 in. (225mm) long.
Ends: ½ × 1 in. (12 × 25mm) softwood, 3 in. (75mm) long.
Blocks: ½ × 2 in. (12 × 50mm) hardwood, 1 in. (25mm) long.

Shooting Board

The shooting board is an invaluable aid for planing end grain without splitting it and for planing the edges of pieces of wood too small to be held against a bench stop or in a vise. Block A is held in the vice at the front of the bench and keeps the board steady while it is used. B is the base of the shooting board, along which the plane is run with its sole against the edge of C. The wood to be planed is rested on C, and is pressed hard up against block D, which acts in much the same way as the block on a bench

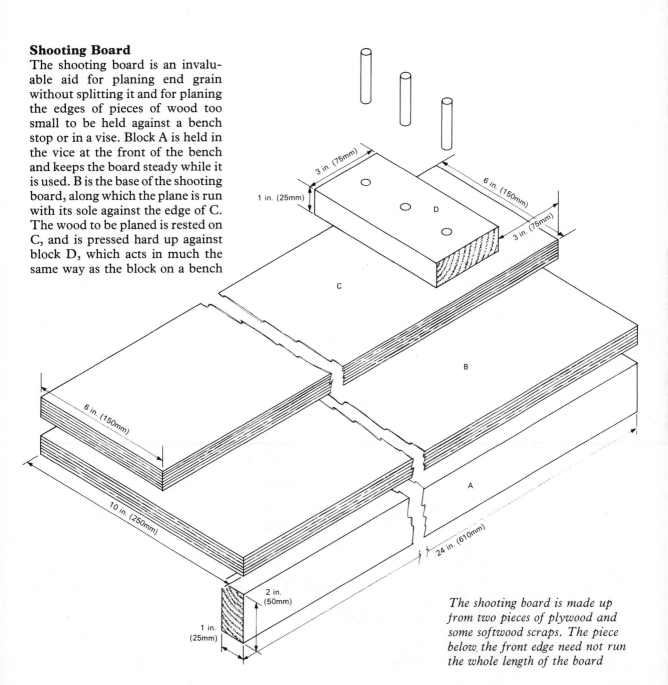

3 in. (75mm)

6 in. (150mm)

1 in. (25mm)

3 in. (75mm)

D

C

6 in. (150mm)

B

10 in. (250mm)

A

24 in. (610mm)

2 in. (50mm)

1 in. (25mm)

The shooting board is made up from two pieces of plywood and some softwood scraps. The piece below the front edge need not run the whole length of the board

151

hook. It must be exactly square to the edge of C.

The overall length of the shooting board can be between about 18 in. (457mm) and as much as 3 ft. (915mm), although a length of around 24 in. (610mm) will be ideal for most bench work. For this design the best materials to use are ½ in. (12mm) plywood for the base B and support C, and softwood for blocks A and D. A is a piece of 1 × 2 in (25 × 50mm) softwood doweled and glued to the underside of B. B measures 10 × 24 in. (250 × 610mm), while C is the same length but only 6 in. (150mm) wide. Block D measures 6 × 3 × 1 in. (150 × 75 × 25mm), and is glued and doweled into place about 3 in. (75mm) from the end of the shooting board, to allow the plane

to run on after planing the wood held against D.

B and C can be simply glued together and weighted or clamped until the glue has set. Then the position of D is marked on C with the try square held against the edge of C, so that it is fixed at an exact right angle to the edge of C.

Cutting list for shooting board

A 1 × 2 in. (25 × 50mm) softwood, 24 in. (610mm) long
B ½ in. (12mm) plywood, 10 × 24 in. (250 × 610).
C ½ in. (12mm) plywood, 6 × 24 in. (150 × 610mm).
D 1 × 3 in. (25 × 75mm) softwood, 6 in. (150mm) long.
Dowel 2 in. (50mm) long, ⅜ in. (9mm) in diameter.

Slot-together sawhorse

For sawing up large boards, or cutting pieces off long lengths of wood, a couple of sawhorses will come in extremely handy. The carpenter usually makes them up on site from scraps of rough wood, but here's an attractive design that you can make to keep in the shop. It has the advantage that it can be dismantled and put away neatly when it is not needed—a great help in a small workshop.

It is made entirely from ½ in. (12mm) thick plywood, cut out in the two shapes and sizes shown opposite. You will need two of each piece. When all the pieces have been cut out, mark each one up for the grooves that will allow the two cross pieces to be slotted into the legs. Each slot is 3 in. (75mm) deep and ½ in. (12mm) wide. Those in the legs are cut at right angles to the top edge, while those in the cross pieces are cut at an angle as shown. It is easier to find the slot position in this way than by a lot of complicated geometry. The slots are cut down with a coping saw, and then chiseled out neatly at the end. They should be a tight fit when interlocked as the saw horse will wobble if they're not cut sufficiently tight.

Round off the corners of each cross piece, and the top corners of each leg. When you assemble the sawhorse for use, tap the interlocking parts together with a mallet or a piece of scrap wood and knock them gently apart again when you've finished.

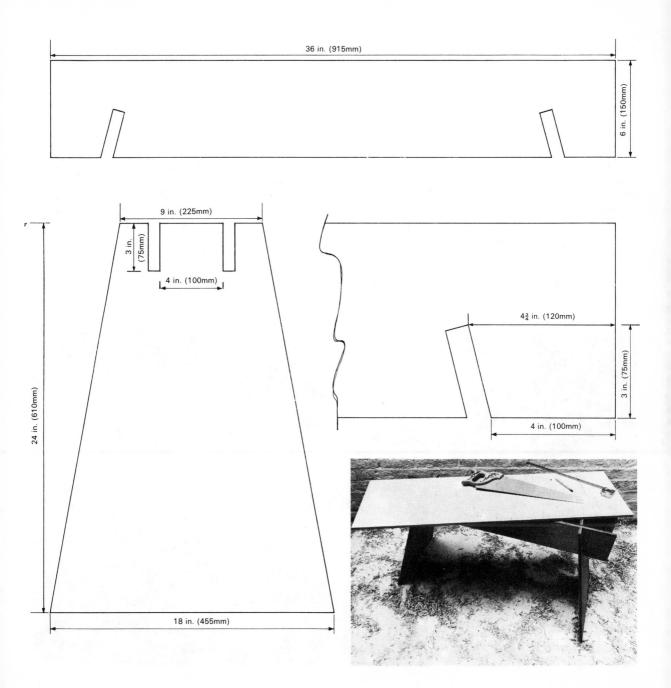

36 in. (915mm)

6 in. (150mm)

9 in. (225mm)

3 in. (75mm)

4 in. (100mm)

24 in. (610mm)

18 in. (455mm)

4¾ in. (120mm)

3 in. (75mm)

4 in. (100mm)

A workbench

The last—and perhaps the most vital—piece of equipment you can make for your workshop is a workbench. Here is a design for one which is easy to make *without* a bench because it uses standard sizes of wood and sheet material that you can order ready cut from your supplier. All you will have to do is clean up the edges and put all the pieces together.

As you can see from the first drawing it's a traditional type of bench with sturdy legs, overhanging front and ends so you can attach a portable vise or use clamps to hold your work firmly, a well in which to keep the tools you're using, and a rack at the back for other tools you want on hand during the job.

It measures 48 in. (1220mm) long and 24 in. (610mm) deep—big enough for most woodworking jobs—and can be made to suit your height simply by varying the length of the legs. The apron and shelf help to brace the structure securely, yet they can be easily unscrewed if the bench has to be dismantled at any time. The top is held on by screws and angle brackets for the same reason, and to

make the bench more versatile there's the option of having the top hinged in two parts so the bench can be converted into a table for hobbies and the like.

The first stage in making the bench is to assemble the two end frames. Each of these consists of two legs about 2 in. (50mm) shorter than the overall height of the bench, and two side rails that are bolted to the inside faces of the legs. Begin by marking and cutting the lower end of the four legs exactly square. Then measure along each leg the length you want, mark and cut squarely again. Do

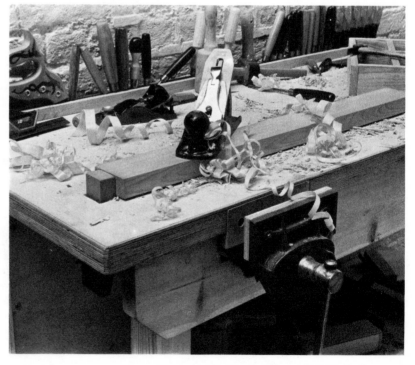

Above: the work surface folded to form the well; tools are within easy reach in the rack along the back. Right: for some jobs a flat, continuous work surface is needed, so the hinged worktop is folded back into the well

154

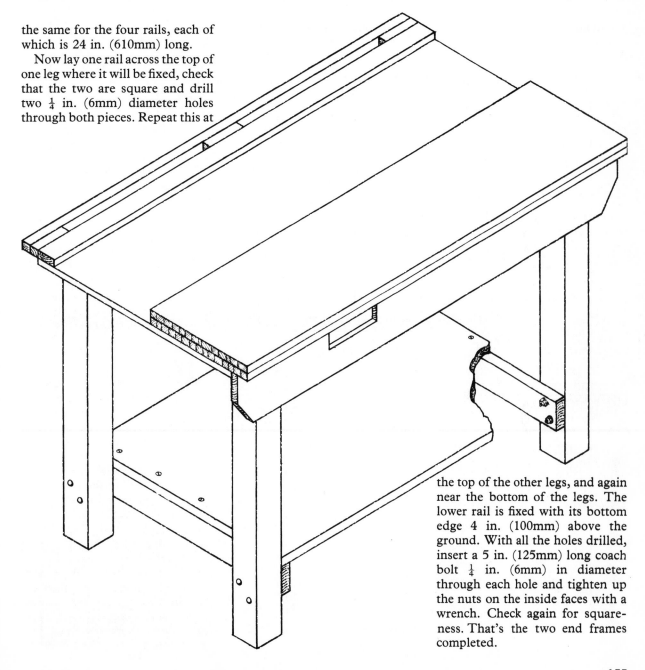

the same for the four rails, each of which is 24 in. (610mm) long.

Now lay one rail across the top of one leg where it will be fixed, check that the two are square and drill two $\frac{1}{4}$ in. (6mm) diameter holes through both pieces. Repeat this at the top of the other legs, and again near the bottom of the legs. The lower rail is fixed with its bottom edge 4 in. (100mm) above the ground. With all the holes drilled, insert a 5 in. (125mm) long coach bolt $\frac{1}{4}$ in. (6mm) in diameter through each hole and tighten up the nuts on the inside faces with a wrench. Check again for square- ness. That's the two end frames completed.

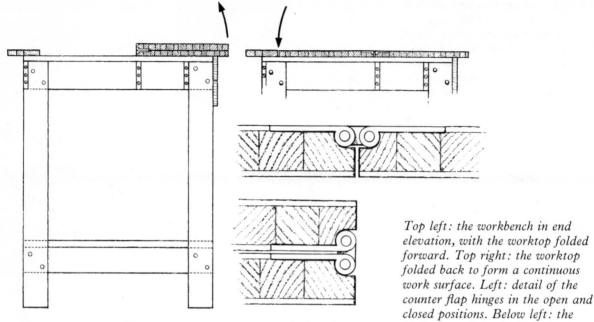

Top left: the workbench in end elevation, with the worktop folded forward. Top right: the worktop folded back to form a continuous work surface. Left: detail of the counter flap hinges in the open and closed positions. Below left: the front view of the workbench

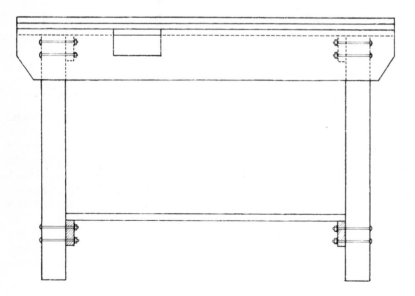

The working area of the bench is 12 in. (305mm) wide, and consists of two pieces of $\frac{3}{4}$ in. (18mm) blockboard. These can be either glued together to form a solid top $1\frac{1}{2}$ in. (38mm) thick or they can be hinged together with four counter flap hinges so that the upper part can be folded back into the well of the bench to create a flat table top.

Forming the well of the bench and running below the blockboard work surface is a sheet of $\frac{3}{4}$ in. (18mm) thick chipboard measuring 24 × 48 in. (610 × 1220mm). This in turn rests on the two end frames, and is secured to them by the angle brackets mentioned earlier. The tool rack is fixed along the rear edge of the chipboard. This rack consists of two long pieces of softwood, separated by three spacer blocks at about 18 in. (457mm) intervals to form slots into which your tools can be placed while you're working.

Take the piece of chipboard and mark two lines on it, one 2 in. (50mm) from the rear edge and the other 10 in. (250mm) from the front edge. The first line marks where the tool rack will go. This is made up before being fixed in place. The other marks where the blockboard work surface fits.

If you want the solid work surface, glue and clamp the two pieces of blockboard firmly together, and leave to set before cleaning up the sawn edges. Then attach the composite board to the chipboard by driving 1½ in. (38mm) screws through the chipboard into it, having drilled pilot and clearance holes first. Glue the two together as well for extra strength.

If you prefer the hinged work surface, fix the two blockboard leaves together first with four counter hinges, spacing the hinges about 12 in. (305mm) apart. Then attach the lower part to the chipboard in the same way as before, but use 1¼ in. (32mm) screws instead so they penetrate just the one piece of blockboard. Check that the upper piece folds back flat over what will be the well of the bench. Then you can attach the tool rack to the rear edge of the chipboard with screws driven up

through the chipboard into the wider part of the rack. That completes the top of the bench.

The next job is to attach it to the side frames, using three 3 in. (75mm) metal angle brackets at each side. These are screwed to the inside faces of the upper side rails. Two are positioned below the work surface and the third below the tool rack, so that the fixing screws can pass right through the chipboard to hold the whole top firmly in place.

The shelf that rests on the lower side rails can now be cut and screwed down to the rails. It measures 24 × 36 in. (610 × 915mm) Finally, the apron is added across the front of the bench and is screwed into place to the legs

at each end. Its lower corners are cut off at an angle, and there is a cut-out in it to allow a portable vise to be attached, or you can fit a proper bench-mounted vise here instead, screwing it to packing pieces on the underside of the bench top.

If you want bench stops, simply chop square holes through the blockboard work surface but not through the chipboard below, and drop in square hardwood bench stops when you need them. However, this works only with the solid work surface. With the hinged one the holes will mar its appearance. In this case a piece of wood clamped across the bench will serve instead.

Cutting list for workbench

Legs:	3 in. (75mm) sq. softwood	30 in. (760mm) long
Rails:	1 × 3 in. (25 × 75mm) softwood	24 in. (610mm) long
Top:	¾ in. (18mm) chipboard	24 × 48 in. (610 × 1220mm)
Work surfaces:	¾ in. (18mm) blockboard	12 × 48 in. (305 × 1220mm)
Shelf:	¾ in. (18mm) chipboard	24 × 36 in. (610 × 915mm)
Apron:	¾ in. (18mm) chipboard	6 × 48 in. (150 × 1220mm)
Tool rack:	¾ × 2 in. (18 × 50mm) softwood	48 in (1220mm) long
	¾ × 1 in. (18 × 25mm) softwood	54 in. (1370mm) long

Hardware

Four counter hinges: 1 × 3 in. (25 × 75mm)
Sixteen coach bolts and nuts: 5 in. (125mm) long and ¼ in. (6mm) in diameter
Six metal angle brackets, 3 in. (75mm) long
Assorted countersunk screws

Glossary

Architrave: decorative molding framing a door or window

Arris: sharp edge or corner of a piece of wood

Astragal: type of molding

Auger: formerly a boring tool with a long shank ending in a screw point, with a handle at right angles; now a type of bit

Awl: small sharp-pointed tool used mainly for making small pilot holes in wood

Baluster: short, often molded pillar, supporting a handrail

Band saw: powered saw driving a continuous saw blade, rather like a tape cartridge

Batten: piece of wood used to support a framework or panel, particularly attached to a wall

Beading: molding of small cross section, usually used for decoration

Bevel: tool for setting angles, also a sloping edge or surface on wood or on a tool blade

Birdsmouth: type of molding

Carcass: framework, usually of rough wood which will be paneled in and hidden

Casement: hinged part of window

Castor: small wheel on mounting, attached to underside of furniture to make it mobile

Chamfer: symmetrical (45°) bevel planed on an edge of a piece of wood

Clearance hole: hole drilled in wood to accept the shank of a screw

Clench nailing: nailing technique where nail points are driven through wood and then doubled back into the wood again

Combination plane: plane with interchangeable cutters for making grooves, rabbets, moldings and the like

Compass saw: a thin-bladed saw, used for cutting small holes in wood; also called a keyhole or pad saw

Countersink: conical hole drilled to accept screw head, using special countersinking bit

Dado: in England, the lower part of a room wall, often paneled in wood; in America, a housing

Double tenon: tenon on wide wood, cut in two parts so that wide, weak mortise is not required

End grain: the grain exposed when wood is cut across the grain; poor at holding screws and difficult to glue successfully

Escutcheon: small plate used to cover keyhole, fixed with round-headed escutcheon pins

Face side, face edge: prepared side or edge of wood from which measurements are taken and joints marked out

Feather-edge board: board cut in a wedge shape, thinner along one edge than the other

Fence: guide attached to plane or power saw to guide tool a fixed distance from the edge of the workpiece

Figure: the grain pattern of the wood as exposed by sawing

Flat-sawn: wood cut from the log by a series of parallel cuts

Gimlet: boring tool like small auger, but with wooden handle

Glazing bar: specially-shaped molding holding window panes

Grinding angle: angle ground on blade of plane or chisel, from which the cutting edge is sharpened

Groove: channel cut along the length of a piece of wood, parallel with the grain direction

Honing: sharpening plane or chisel blade to the honing angle, slightly greater than the grinding angle

Isometric drawing: form of working drawing where all lengths are true scale lengths, verticals are drawn vertical and horizontals at an angle of 30°

Kerf: cut made by saw teeth, slightly wider than the saw blade due to the set of the teeth

Key: roughening of adjacent surfaces prior to gluing, to improve adhesion

Knotting: sealer applied over knots to prevent resin bleeding through into paint film

Lath: thin section of wood used for trelliswork and as a support for plaster in lath-and-plaster walls and ceilings

Melamine: type of plastic, used as facing material in plastic-coated chipboard and as melamine-formaldehyde resin, in making plastic laminates

Miter: cut made at 45° across a piece of wood; two miters butted together form a miter joint

Mortise: slot cut in wood to accept tenon, lock or other hardware

Molding: wood machined into special profiles rather than simple square, rectangular or round cross-sections

Mullion: upright separating the fixed lights and casements in a window frame

Paring: shaving away wood with a chisel, usually across the grain

Pilot hole: hole drilled in wood to accept the threaded part of a screw and make driving it easier

Plastic laminate: surfacing material made up from layers of paper impregnated with special resins and pressed into a durable sheet

Plastic wood: pliable wood stopper used to fill holes and cracks in wood

Polyurethane: type of resin used in paints and varnishes to produce a hard-wearing surface

Points per inch (ppi): the number of complete teeth per inch on a saw blade, a measure of its fineness (and speed) of cut

Preservative: chemical used to treat wood in order to make it resistant to insect and fungal attack

PVA glue (white glue): woodworking adhesive, an emulsion of polyvinyl acetate in water

Quadrant: molding like a quarter circle in cross-section

Quarter-sawn: wood cut from the log in cuts along the radius, like slices of a cake

Rabbet/rebate: step-shaped cutout along one edge of a piece of wood into which another piece (or in a framework, a panel) fits

Sash: sliding part of a sash window (cf. casement)

Scribing: marking a piece of wood to match exactly the contours of another surface against which it must fit exactly

Set: the bending of saw teeth alternately to one side or the other along the blade

Shiplap: type of cladding machined so that successive pieces overlap one another

Shoulder: step cut at end of wood to expose end grain, as in a tenon

Skew nailing: driving nails at an angle into the wood surface

Stile: upright member of door or window casement

Stopped joint: joint where mortise or housing does not completely pass through the member in which it is cut

Tang: point of a tool onto which a wooden or plastic handle fits

Tenon: tongue cut on the end of one member, intended to fit into a mortise cut in the other

Through joint: joint where mortise or housing passes right through the member in which it is cut (cf. stopped joint)

Tongue-and-groove joint: edge-to-edge joint where a tongue is machined on the edge of one piece of wood to fit into a matching groove cut in the other

Twist drill: boring device with round shank, used in hand or power drills

Veneer: thin layer of wood with decorative grain pattern, stuck onto plainer and usually less expensive wood surface

Waney edge: bark-covered edge of a piece of wood cut from the outside of the log

Warp: twist in wood, caused by uneven seasoning or improper storage

Metric measurements are fine if you are used to them, confusing otherwise. Don't be afraid of them: they're much more accurate than standard measurements and fractions and much easier to add and subtract. Get a dual-marked tape measure and get used to them now. The world is soon going to be all metric, whether we like it or not.

Rather than give you reams of conversion tables, I thought I would end simply by reminding you of a few rough conversions.

One inch is about **25 millimeters** (so four inches is 100mm, one foot is about 300mm and so on). For really accurate conversions use 1 in. = 25.4mm—on your calculator.

One meter is about **3 ft. 3 in.**

One square meter equals about **1.2 sq. yd.**

One cubic meter equals about **$1\frac{1}{3}$ cu. yd.**

One liter is about **$1\frac{3}{4}$ pints** (UK), **2.1 pints** (US)

One kilogram is about **2.2 lbs.** For accurate work, use conversion tables.

Index